Straight from the heart

'I have you in my heart ... all of you share in God's grace with me'
Philippians 1:1

Selwyn Hughes & Philip Greenslade
Revised and updated by Mick Brooks
FURTHER STUDY: IAN SEWTER

© CWR 2015. Dated text previously published as *Every Day with Jesus: Joy: The Serious Business of Heaven* (March/April 2001) by CWR. This edition revised and updated for 2016 by Mick Brooks.

CWR, Waverley Abbey House, Waverley Lane, Farnham, Surrey GU9 8EP, UK **Tel: 01252 784700**
Email: mail@cwr.org.uk Registered Charity No. 294387. Registered Limited Company No. 1990308.

Cover image: getty.com/Stepan Popov
Quiet Time image: fotosearch.com
Printed in England by Linney Print

MIX
Paper from responsible sources
FSC® C015900
www.fsc.org

Every Day with Jesus is available in **large print** from CWR. It is also available on **audio and DAISY** in the UK and Eire for the sole use of those with a visual impairment worse than N12, or who are registered blind. For details please contact **Torch Trust for the Blind**, Tel: 01858 438260. Torch Trust for the Blind, Torch House, Torch Way, Northampton Road, Market Harborough LE16 9HL.

A word of introduction ...

There is always, despite it fast becoming a dying art, something exciting about receiving a handwritten letter. Opening the envelope, holding the textured paper, seeing the ink and distinctive handwriting; these all make for such a personal experience of reading. Although amazingly instant, I think something of the personal touch is inevitably lost in email. The truth of Proverbs 25:25 ('like cold water to a weary soul is good news from a distant land') couldn't have been more true and real when living overseas with my family. So much so, that it became a daily family ritual to walk out to check the post-box, hoping for news and encouragement.

Paul's letter to the Philippians helps us to understand the gospel as a gospel of love: not just receiving love but sharing love too. Paul is not only able to expound and live the love of God from his prison cell, he also reaches out in love and encouragement. This deeply personal letter, so clearly written from Paul's heart, shows how we can learn to live with almost anything: suffering, disappointments and the many, various curve balls life throws in our direction. The reality is that no matter what we are facing – personal struggles, circumstances beyond our control or the consequences of poor choices – we *can* face these issues. It is so much easier to face difficulties if we know we are not alone, that somebody cares enough to journey alongside us.

I hope that these devotionals will encourage you in love for God and those God has put around you. You might even consider writing and sending a personal letter of encouragement letter to someone today.

Mick Brooks, Consulting Editor

You're a saint!

TUES
1 MAR

FOR READING & MEDITATION - PHILIPPIANS 1:1

'Paul and Timothy, servants of Christ Jesus, to all the saints in Christ
Jesus at Philippi' (v1)

Our meditations in this issue take us on a journey through
the epistle to the Philippians. Dr Cynddylan Jones, a
great Welsh commentator, called it 'the Epistle of Joy'.
Certainly it is one of Paul's most affectionate and intimate
letters.

The manner of Paul's opening shows us something of the
revolution the gospel had brought about in the area of human
relationships. In society in general far too often leaders
lord it over those under them, but the gospel reverses this.
Here two leaders in the Early Church – Paul and Timothy
– see themselves as 'servants' writing to meet
the needs of the saints! It is Jesus, of course, who
makes this difference. In His light, social status is
turned upside down. Measured by Him we are all
'bondservants' whatever 'leadership' position we
hold in the Church.

Paul's opening greeting is first to the 'saints in
Christ Jesus at Philippi'. So often we tend to think
of saints as people who have been canonised and
whose faces are set in stained-glass windows. But
in scripture saints are ordinary people: merchants,
builders, tentmakers, home-makers, and so on.
Anyone who is 'in Christ' is a saint. The people
whom Paul was addressing had a dual citizenship:
'*in* Christ' and 'at Philippi'. Their homes were in Philippi but
their true lives were found in Jesus. 'Where do you live?' an
elderly Scottish Christian was asked. With a twinkle in his
eye he replied: 'I have my abode at Edinburgh but I *live* in
Christ.' Christians are indeed a rare breed – the only people
to live in two places at once. So keep in mind that in the eyes
of Jesus we are all saints. The challenge lies in living as such.

**FURTHER
STUDY**

Rom. 1:7;
Eph. 1:1;
1 Cor. 1:1-2;
2 Cor. 1:1

1. What qualifies
you to be
a saint?

2. What is
the address
of a saint?

**Father, help me live as a saint should live - to be committed,
dedicated, free from sin and wholly caught up in You. The standard
is high but Your power is unlimited. Fill me with that power and
flow through me to others. Amen.**

What a letter opening!

FOR READING & MEDITATION - PHILIPPIANS 1:2

'Grace and peace to you from God our Father and the
Lord Jesus Christ.' (v2)

Traditionally, as you probably know, conventional greetings began where we end – with the signature. All historical letters (even secular letters) began by the sender identifying both himself (or herself) and the recipient, together with a wish for good health. Paul's opening salutation, however, is different. He fills it with Christian content, and the usual wish for good health is transformed into a blessing: 'Grace and peace to you from God our Father and the Lord Jesus Christ.'

Jesus Christ transforms everything He touches – even letter openings. In Jesus our 'hellos' can be so much more than mere greetings; they impart grace and bestow peace. As followers of Jesus, when writing on a friendly basis to one another (or even sending emails) we can seek to bless each other with words that reflect our wish for spiritual prosperity. The phrase 'Grace and peace to you' is not a greeting-card message, but one with deep spiritual content. As in all his other correspondence, Paul invests his greeting with the substance of what he intends to say and expand upon in the rest of the letter. Already he has emphasised that the Christians at Philippi are saints, and now he foreshadows the message of grace and peace that he will go on to show is the basis of their fellowship in Jesus.

Paul's wish for the Philippians is that they will receive not only grace, but grace *and* peace. Grace oils the wheels of life, and peace makes the ride more pleasant. And notice they come from 'God our Father'. Grace and peace could come from nowhere else. Isn't it amazing what can be got out of a welcome and 'hello'?

FURTHER STUDY

1 Cor. 1:3-9;
Eph. 1:2-14

1. How has God blessed us with grace?

2. How are grace and peace related?

Father, make me more sensitive to the needs of my brothers and sisters, and help me not simply to communicate with them but to minister to them. You minister so graciously to me; teach me how to minister graciously to others. Amen.

Thanks for the memory!

FOR READING & MEDITATION – PHILIPPIANS 1:3

'I thank my God every time I remember you.' (v3)

The letter to the Philippians must be the most famous 'thank you' note in history! There were several reasons why Paul put pen to parchment and wrote to the Philippians, but one of his primary reasons was to thank them for their continued sponsorship of his ministry. But notice that he not only thanks *them* but thanks *God* for them. Every time the Philippian Christians came to mind, he offered thanks to the Lord for them. What a tremendous way to remember people.

The great preacher C.H. Spurgeon once said: 'There must be "think" at the bottom of "thank".' By that he meant that there ought to be an intelligent content to our thanksgiving. How wonderful it would be if whenever someone's name popped into our mind – that of a person for whom we had a special reason to be thankful – the memory triggered us to offer prayerful thanksgiving for them. One preacher suggests all Christians ought to keep a 'journal of thankfulness', in which the names of those who have brought a special blessing into their lives are recorded. 'Go over the list occasionally,' he advises, 'and as gratitude rises for what they have done for you, let that gratitude rise also to God.' He adds: 'It is the best way I know of cultivating an attitude of gratitude and appreciation.'

But it would be more wonderful still if we not only thanked God for them, but prayed for them too. The most joyous Christians are those who turn everything to prayer and praise. Does anyone come to mind at this moment who has been a special blessing in your life? Have you thanked them? If not, do so today. Thank God for them too, and offer up a prayer for them.

FURTHER STUDY

Col. 1:2-14;
1 Thess. 1:1-3;
2 Thess. 1:1-4

1. How does thankfulness cultivate gratitude?

2. How was Paul's thanking based on his thinking?

Father, forgive me that I take so many things for granted. Thank You for all the good things You have done for me, are doing now and will do in the future. Help me to be thankful to others who bless me – and to say so. Amen.

Joy - our prerogative

FOR READING & MEDITATION - PHILIPPIANS 1:4

'In all my prayers for all of you, I always pray with joy' (v4)

Paul tells us in the verse before us today that every time he prays for the Philippians he prays 'with joy'. This is the first time Paul mentions the word 'joy' in his epistle but, as we shall see, the word will appear many more times. If, as it has been said, the New Testament is the 'most joyful book in the world' then the letter to the Philippians is the most joyful epistle in that book. Joy is a theme that dominates this great letter of Paul's, and the atmosphere of joy is all-pervasive and contagious. But what is joy and where does it come from? Some distinctions are called for.

FURTHER STUDY

Psa. 16:1-11;
Isa. 12:1-6;
Rom. 14:17

1. Define joy.

2. What is the source of joy?

Joy is quite different from pleasure, for example. Pleasure comes to us usually from things that affect our senses: a beautiful sunset, a brilliant painting, a son or daughter's wedding, the birth of a child, fine dining and so on. But all these things are vulnerable to disappointment, even tragedy and loss. Joy, the joy that comes from God, however, is something that can never be taken from us. Pleasure most often depends on circumstances. It can be stolen from us (temporarily at least) by minor irritations, such as a toothache or seasickness. In contrast, joy, Christian joy – the joy that flows into our hearts (if we let it) by the Holy Spirit – is independent of circumstances.

Again, pleasures come and go. What pleases the youth doesn't please the man. The joy of God, though, is constant. It rises to rise again. Joy is deep. The smile is not only on the lips, but in the heart. It may flame up into rapture or sink into peace. 'Joy,' said C.S. Lewis, 'is the serious business of heaven.'* It ought to be the serious business of earth too.

Father, how can I sufficiently thank You for the joy that You have deposited in my soul? It is too good to keep to myself. Grant that it may overflow from me to others. In Jesus' name. Amen.

* From *Letters to Malcolm: Chiefly on Prayer.* © Copyright CS Lewis Pte Ltd.

CWR Ministry Events
PLEASE PRAY FOR THE TEAM

DATE	EVENT	PLACE	PRESENTER(S)
3 Mar	Decision Making and the Will of God	Waverley Abbey House	Andy Peck
7-11 Mar	Introduction to Biblical Care and Counselling	Pilgrim Hall	John Munt and Team
10 Mar	Discovering Your Spiritual Gifts	WAH	Andy Peck
10 Mar	The Bible in an Evening	WAH	Andy Peck
11-13 Mar	Bible Discovery Weekend: Jesus and the New Covenant (from Passover to Pentecost)	WAH	Philip Greenslade
16 Mar	Inspiring Women Spring Day: What does the Bible actually say about women?	WAH	Elizabeth Hodkinson
17 Mar	Preachers' Workshop	WAH	Andy Peck
22 Mar	Passover Supper	WAH	Elizabeth Hodkinson
1 Apr-7 May	Certificate in Counselling Supervision	PH	Heather Churchill
14 Apr	Pastoring through Life's Crises	WAH	Andy Peck
15-17 Apr	Inspiring Women Spring Weekend: Discovering the Beauty Within	WAH	Ros Derges, Rosie Morgan and Lynette Brooks
15 Apr	Structuring Pastoral Care	WAH	Andy Peck
27 Apr	Understanding Yourself, Understanding Others	WAH	Jeannette Barwick

Please pray for our students and tutors on our ongoing BA Counselling programme at Waverley and Pilgrim Hall, as well as our Certificate and Diploma of Christian Counselling and MA in Christian Counselling qualifications.

We would also appreciate prayer for our ministry in Singapore as well as our many regional events that we are embarking on this year.

For further information and a full list of CWR's courses, phone **+44 (0)1252 784719** or visit the CWR website **www.cwr.org.uk**

You can also download our free daily Prayer Track from **www.cwr.org.uk/free-resources**

Shareholders in the gospel

FOR READING & MEDITATION – PHILIPPIANS 1:5

'because of your partnership in the gospel from the first day
until now' (v5)

Paul tells us in this verse why his prayers for the
Philippians were filled with joy. It was because of their
'partnership in the gospel from the first day until now'. The
word 'partnership' is a translation from the Greek word
koinonia, which is sometimes translated 'fellowship' or
'communion'. This beautiful Greek word does not suggest
a warm fuzzy feeling generated by a social event or even a
time of worship. The word implies a share in something; to
hold something in common – whether an experience or an
activity. When Christians share together they are not just
sharing with each other but sharing together in the
Father, Son and Holy Spirit.

FURTHER STUDY

1 Cor. 3:5-10;
2 Cor. 8:1-5;
11:9

1. In what way
were Paul
and Apollos
partners?

2. How can we
be partners in
the gospel?

Koinonia was coined by Greek wordsmiths to
describe those in business partnerships, and implies
bonds of commitment and co-operation. This is no
doubt the meaning Paul had in mind when he used
the word here. The Christian community in Philippi
were Paul's partners in the gospel – his long-term
sponsors who had helped to underwrite some of
his apostolic missions. The Philippians had taken
out shares in the cause of the gospel.

Permit a personal question: Have you taken
out shares in the cause of the gospel? Are you
committed to supporting some special project
designed to bring people to Jesus or help believers go deeper
with God? Your local church, of course, is where your
first responsibility lies, but those whom God has blessed
financially can spread their resources wider. And those with
limited financial resources can still be partners in prayer.
CWR only exists today because of such partnerships. And
even the great apostle Paul could not have accomplished the
things he did had he not had his partners.

**Loving heavenly Father, help me review my investments in Your
kingdom. Show me how I can best empower others through my
prayers and my giving. Guide me in this, dear Lord, for I want my
investments to yield the greatest rewards. Amen.**

God's cause never fails

FOR READING & MEDITATION - PHILIPPIANS 1:6

'being confident of this, that he who began a good work in you will carry it on to completion until the day of Christ Jesus.' (v6)

Dr Martyn Lloyd-Jones, the famous expositor who once occupied the pulpit of Westminster Chapel, London, disliked the idea of Christians having favourite texts. However, on one occasion he confessed that if pressed to select one, the text before us today would be his choice. The thought that captivated Martyn Lloyd-Jones, and came out often in his preaching, was that the God who begins a good work in us will always carry it through to completion. This was another reason why Paul could pray with joy – he was free from the fear that God's cause would fail. Coventry Patmore, a nineteenth-century poet, said: 'All realities sing – and nothing else will.' With his piercing perception of spiritual matters, not unlike that of his Master, Paul saw reality – the reality that nothing could successfully work against the plans and purposes of God. He saw reality – and sang!

The 'good work' that God began in the lives of the Philippians might be their support for Paul and his ministry, but the mention of 'the day of Christ Jesus' makes it more likely that it was the saving work of grace that began in their lives when they responded in repentant faith to the preaching of the gospel. Of course, the good work the Philippians were doing in supporting Paul's mission was in itself evidence of the bigger work of grace in their lives.

Treasure this thought: God completes what He begins. The Almighty never grows weary of well doing. Do you feel you are in the middle of one of God's 'slow movements' right now? Remember that even in our times of waiting, as well as our wanderings, failures and stubbornness, He composes no unfinished symphonies. What He starts He completes.

FURTHER STUDY

Ruth 1:1-2:3; 4:13-21

1. How did God complete His work in Ruth?

2. What part did Ruth play?

Father, what encouragement it gives me to know that You never start anything unless You can see it through. This means You will not give up on me - difficult and unworthy though I am. Thank You my Father. Thank You. Amen.

Completion Day

FOR READING & MEDITATION - PHILIPPIANS 1:6

'being confident of this, that he who began a good work in you will carry it on to completion until the day of Christ Jesus.' (v6)

We spend another day on this sixth verse, reflecting this time on the fact that He who has begun a good work in us will carry it on to completion 'until the day of Christ Jesus'. Drop your anchor into the depths of this reassuring and encouraging revelation right now: God does not allow the work He has begun in you to be thwarted. What a basis for confidence. Our human decisions alone would provide too shaky a basis for trust, but the unshakeable resolution of God gives us eternal hope. 'Our ultimate salvation,' says the Christian writer Alec Motyer, 'can be no more forfeited than the Father can break off His pledged promise to glorify His Son in the day of Christ.'

FURTHER STUDY

Eph. 5:25-32;
Rev. 19:5-9;
21:1-7

1. How will you appear on completion day?

2. What gives us eternal hope?

Most, no doubt, will be familiar with John Bunyan's *Pilgrim's Progress*. When the main character, Christian, saw water being poured on the fire against the wall in that timeless story, he initially feared the work of grace would be extinguished by the devil. But his wonder grew when he saw how the flames burned hotter and hotter. Then he was shown the other side of the wall, where a man with a vessel of oil in his hand secretly and continually cast oil on the fire. This, it was explained to him, 'was Christ who continually with the oil of grace maintains the work already begun in the heart'.

There is for us all a day of completion – a deadline, if we can call it that – the day of Christ. For all those willing to give themselves to God's dealings it will not just be a judgment day but a glorious day of completion and consummation – a wonderful parade of those to whom God will apply the finishing touches. Hallelujah!

Father God, my joy knows no bounds as I realise the work of grace that You are achieving in my life cannot be extinguished by the devil. What confidence it gives me to know I am in good hands - Your hands. Reign in me, dear Father. Amen.

A new life – a new love

FOR READING & MEDITATION – PHILIPPIANS 1:7

'I have you in my heart; for whether I am in chains or defending and confirming the gospel, all of you share in God's grace with me.' (v7)

Paul's passion for the gospel it seems is matched only by his affection for the Philippians. Although the great apostle is in prison as a result of proclaiming the gospel, his feelings are not taken up with his own plight; his heart goes out to the Philippians whom he loves with the affection of Jesus. 'I have you in my heart,' he says.

Paul reveals here that he was not only a worshipping man but also a caring and warm man. One woman who carried in her mind the impression of Paul as being cold and hard tells how her opinion changed dramatically when she realised how devoted Paul was to the people at Philippi. 'I began,' she said, 'to have great affection for the man who gave his life for Jesus.' The apostle does not put himself on a pedestal but sees his Philippian friends as sharers together in the grace of God. So what turned Paul from being a zealous persecutor of followers of Jesus into a defender and lover of Christian believers?

On the Damascus Road the life of God had come into his life, and when God's life comes in so does His love. You cannot separate God's life from His love, and neither can you separate God's love from His life. When we receive Jesus' life we receive also His love. Have you noticed this to be true? Do you remember how, before you were converted, you had little affection for or interest in Christian people? Perhaps you hoped you would never be associated with such an odd group! But after you knew Jesus, when the life of God came into you, so did His love. Now your greatest friends are found in this community. You have found, as everyone who knows Jesus finds, that when a new life comes in so does a new love.

FURTHER STUDY

Rom. 5:1-5;
8:35-39;
2 Cor. 5:14-15

1. What motivated and strengthened Paul?

2. How did this affect his actions?

Yes, Father, it is true – when Your life came into my life so also did Your love. Forgive me if I am allowing anything to hinder that love flowing out. From today onwards may Your love flow fully and freely through me. In Jesus' name. Amen.

'Love changes everything'

FOR READING & MEDITATION - PHILIPPIANS 1:8

'God can testify how I long for all of you with the affection of Christ Jesus.' (v8)

Eugene Peterson, in his paraphrase *The Message*, translates verse 8 in this way: 'He knows how much I love and miss you these days. Sometimes I think I feel as strongly about you as Christ does!' Here again we get a glimpse of the deep affection that Paul felt for the Philippian believers. And this affection did not stem from the fact that they had supported him; it was not just prompted by what they had given but who they were in Jesus.

When writing to the Romans Paul said: 'God has poured out his love into our hearts by the Holy Spirit, whom he has given us' (Rom. 5:5). When we come to love Jesus then a surprising thing happens: we begin to love everybody else who Jesus loves. If all Christians loved in the way He loves us what a different place the Church, and the world, would be.

FURTHER STUDY

John 13:1-5, 34-35;
1 John 4:7-21

1. How can we be like Jesus?

2. How can we have a caring and consistent love?

The kind of love Paul had for the Philippians was mindful, grateful and consistent. Is your love like this? Are people in your church thankful for your mindfulness and your consistency? Or are they tired of your mindlessness and inconsistency? Do you show them love one day and bite their heads off another? This is not the kind of Christian life Jesus wants us to live. As Christians, we should be known for our love.

Hymn singing and worship songs have their place, but what the world needs is love – a love that is caring and consistent. If the Christian Church could learn to live out and demonstrate the love that Paul exemplified there would be less need (not no need) for evangelistic outreaches. The world pauses and takes notice when people love. It cannot do otherwise for love changes everything. Everything!

Father, I ask myself: Am I the kind of Christian who sends a glow through others? Or do I spread gloom wherever I go? Make me a more loving person, I pray. Love more powerfully in me and let that love spread out to others. Amen.

Transforming lives through
the Word of God

Every year we receive hundreds of thank you letters from our *Every Day with Jesus* readers in prisons all over the world. We hear testimonies of change, redemption and freedom in Christ as people read and understand God's Word, sometimes for the very first time.

> *'Words don't do justice to my appreciation for* Every Day with Jesus *... not only for the rehabilitation of walking free in my life, but also to realise that even in a prison cell I am free. I came to prison and found freedom in Christ.'*

Please help us continue to support prisoners wrestling with forgiveness and searching for hope by supplying them with more daily Bible reading notes.

'I have you in my heart; for whether I am in chains or defending and confirming the gospel, all of you share in God's grace with me.' (Philippians 1:7)

Thank you for your support and prayers. If you would like to make a donation, please fill in the 'Gift to CWR' section on the order form at the back of this publication, completing the Gift Aid declaration if appropriate.

Loving much - loving well

FOR READING & MEDITATION - PHILIPPIANS 1:9

'And this is my prayer: that your love may abound more and more in knowledge and depth of insight' (v9)

Now we focus on Paul's great prayer for the Philippians. Making known his prayer for the people to whom he was writing was Paul's characteristic way of beginning his letters. It's interesting, however, to see what Paul actually prays for when he addresses the churches. His concern is not for the success of their evangelism or growth in numbers, but that they might *know* God better. Here he prays also that their love might abound more and more or, as Peterson puts it in *The Message*: 'not only love much but well'. What does it mean to love well? It means that even when human love is not flowing to you, you are still so open to God's love that you can give out love although your own heart may be aching for a human response.

FURTHER STUDY

1 Cor. 13:1-13;
1 John 3:1,11-24;

1. List the characteristics of love.

2. How can we truly love one another?

In today's world there are many misconceptions concerning love. The language of love is devalued currency. People use it flippantly, using phrases such as: 'I love my shoes', 'I love my new haircut' or 'I love my football team.' It is also said by many that 'Love is blind.' But God's love is *not* blind. It is a love that overflows in 'knowledge and depth of insight'. God wants our love to be an informed love, a wise love, with a moral quality about it that knows how to love in truth. God's love is not a sudden adrenaline rush. We do not relate to people merely on the level of hormones! The writer G.H. Morrison once observed that you can always tell a person who loves books or flowers by the way they handle them. Similarly you can always tell a person who loves others by the way they treat them. How do you treat people? With unkindness and disrespect or with 'knowledge and depth of insight'? Love well.

Father, Your Word goes like a dart to the heart of my problems. I want to love much and to love well, yet there are struggles within me that hinder. Cleanse me and purify my heart until my love becomes as real and as consistent as Yours. Amen.

Use your head

'so that you may be able to discern what is best and may be pure
and blameless until the day of Christ' (v10)

We continue reflecting on Paul's prayer for the Philippians
– a prayer in which the great apostle asks that their
love may abound more and more in knowledge and that
they will have clear spiritual discernment. Love must be
more than 'sentimental gush'; that is why Paul prays that
they may be able to discern how to love appropriately. In
effect he is saying you need to use your head and test your
feelings so that your love is not mere sentimentalism.

How much Christian work is motivated by a love
that is not wise? There's a profusion of feeling but little
perception. A certain church puts new converts
through a short discipleship programme that
almost invariably results in them going off to
join another church. And why? Because the love
they are shown is the smothering kind that makes
them feel uncomfortable. That church has love,
but little wisdom.

Martyrs, it has been said, are those who
discovered how to differentiate between the
important and the trivial. In other words, they
have the wisdom to know what was worth dying
for. And if love will tell us what's worth dying for,
it will surely guide us into what is worth living for.

Discerning love, says Paul, is 'filled with the fruit
of righteousness'. 'Sun judged' is a term that could be used
here. There is nothing like sunshine to show up the dirt. A
traveller who made a train journey in the British Isles tells
how he noticed the filthiness of the carriage windows when
the sun came out. Obviously, he said, when the rail network
was privatised the filth was left in the public's possession!
Christians can be people who, when the sun shines on them,
the Son shines through them.

FURTHER STUDY

Luke 10:25-37;
Rom. 12:9;
1 Pet. 1:22

1. List the
thoughtful
loving actions of
the Samaritan.

2. How can
love be sincere
and wise?

**Gracious heavenly Father, grant that my love will be of the highest
calibre – a love that knows how to give and when to give. Save
me from smothering people with my love. May it be sincere and
intelligent, not sentimental gush. Amen.**

Everything serves

FOR READING & MEDITATION - PHILIPPIANS 1:12-14

'Now I want you to know, brothers, that what has happened to me has really served to advance the gospel.' (v12)

Paul's imprisonment had the opposite of its intended effect. Instead of the message of the gospel being hindered, it was advanced. All the soldiers who were guarding Paul realised that he was in prison not because of crime but for Jesus. Evidently that piqued their curiosity, and, as a result of their questioning him about why he was there, Paul was able to talk about Jesus.

Paul adds that most of the Christians in Rome who learned how he had used his opportunities to present the gospel in prison were greatly encouraged. They were now speaking out fearlessly for God. This is a reversal of what we might have expected. Some might think that confidence and boldness would have come to other Christians from Paul being delivered from prison. But no – confidence and boldness came because he stayed there. Why was this? Because they saw Paul turn imprisonment to fruitfulness. They probably thought: 'What does it matter if we are shut up in prison if we can talk with our guards and to the other prisoners?'

FURTHER STUDY

Acts 16:16-34;
2 Cor. 12:7-10

1. How did Paul's troubles turn to fruitfulness?

2. How did Paul handle trouble?

Paul had instilled into the first Christians the truth that they could do more with trouble than just endure it; they can use it. How different from the general run of thinking in the Church today. We expect that the good be exempt from suffering. To us God is good if He saves us from trouble. As Christians we cannot expect to be exempt from trouble, but we can expect to be adequate for it. We can take hold of whatever comes, be it bad, good or indifferent, and with God's help transform what might have been a setback into a spring board. Consider: had Paul been set free to preach, we would never have had the letter to the Philippians.

God, how encouraging it is to know that I am free to use everything that comes my way. Because I belong to You I can stand anything that comes because I can use everything that comes. Thank You my Father. Amen.

What an attitude!

FOR READING & MEDITATION - PHILIPPIANS 1:15-18

'It is true that some preach Christ out of envy and rivalry,
but others out of good will.' (v15)

Despite the fact that imprisonment gave Paul an opportunity to share Jesus with the prison guards, he admits his situation was being exploited by his rivals; their empty and competitive spirit drove them to take advantage of his absence to make a name for themselves. *The Message* says: 'It's true that some here preach Christ because with me out of the way, they think they'll step right into the spotlight.' But even this does not appear to have fazed the irrepressible apostle. In Galatians 1:8, however, he displayed a very different attitude when the truth of the gospel was at stake: 'But even if we or an angel from heaven should preach a gospel other than the one we preached to you, let him be eternally condemned!' Competitive preachers Paul would tolerate, but not competing gospels! At least the preachers in Rome were not spreading heresy!

Is someone reading this today who has experienced (or is experiencing now) something similar to what happened to Paul? When you were absent from church for a period of time did someone take the job you were doing? Possibly it was an illness that caused your absence and the person who took over from you doesn't mind letting you know they have assumed your role! Sad to say, there can be unfriendliness even among Christians. There was jealousy in the Early Church and there is jealousy in today's Church too. But jealousy could not be found in Paul's heart. He could have thought about those who were taking advantage of his imprisonment and been resentful of them, but no – he rejoiced. 'Every time one of them opens his mouth,' he says in effect, 'Christ is proclaimed. So I just cheer them on.' Amazing!

FURTHER STUDY

Gen. 4:1-8;
Gal. 5:22-26;
Heb. 12:15

1. What caused the first murder?

2. What can prevent bitterness taking root?

Father, how I wish I could have the same attitude as Paul and be able to put a positive construction on things. Give me this outlook as I go about my tasks day by day. In Jesus' name. Amen.

Continuous rejoicing

FOR READING & MEDITATION - PHILIPPIANS 1:19-20

'through your prayers and the help given by the Spirit of Jesus Christ, what has happened to me will turn out for my deliverance.' (v19)

We continue reflecting on the amazing attitude demonstrated by Paul in prison. Yesterday we left him in a state of rejoicing. Bishop Taylor Smith, a nineteenth-century British Anglican bishop, used to say: 'The Christian is meant to live a life of *continual* rejoicing.' But how is it possible in such a topsy-turvy world as this to continually rejoice? We can do so when we share Paul's conviction that God never stops working out His purposes no matter how things may look to the contrary.

Paul confesses that he is being sustained not only by his strong faith in the continuous activity of God in his life but by the prayers of others also. It was the great John Wesley who said: 'God does nothing redemptively except through prayer.' How important it is therefore that we pray for one another. Our prayers count in God's big scheme of things, usually in ways beyond our knowing. He sovereignly interweaves our intercession and His intervention into the final tapestry of His strategic purposes. How He does this is the miracle of His grace. Clearly Paul was greatly encouraged through the prayers of the Christians in Philippi.

The British missionary Geoffrey Bull, imprisoned by the Chinese communists in 1950, wrote in his book *God Holds the Key*, 'How is it that so many saints down the years have been able to live in triumph behind bars? It is because they have discovered the secret of freedom ... It is in the conscious co-operation with the living God in the fulfilment of the pure design for which He made us.' Paul couldn't be sure that he would get out of prison alive but he was sure of this: no matter what, Jesus would be glorified.

FURTHER STUDY

Gen. 37:5-11,28,36; 39:1-23; 41:25,39-43; 50:18-21

1. How was God continuously active in Joseph's life?

2. Why could Joseph live in triumph behind bars?

Father I am so grateful for the truth You have brought before me today, namely that You are continually working out Your purposes in my life, no matter how dark and difficult things may be. May this truth be burned deeply into me. Amen.

Either way - we win

FOR READING & MEDITATION - PHILIPPIANS 1:21
'For to me, to live is Christ and to die is gain.' (v21)

Christmas Evans, a great Welsh revivalist, once preached a sermon on this text in which he visualised himself paying a visit to the imperial palace in ancient Rome. He stops before Nero's throne and asks: 'What does it mean for you to live – really live?' Nero answers: 'For me to live is *power.*' Next he crosses to one of Rome's magnificent libraries, and seeing the philosopher, Seneca, sitting before an old manuscript asks him the same question: 'What does it mean for you to live?' The philosopher knits his brow and says: 'For me to live is *thought.*' Then he goes to the prison where Paul is incarcerated, and stopping before the great apostle asks: 'And what does it mean for you to live?' The prisoner's face brightens as he replies: 'For me to live is *Christ.*' Then he adds: 'And to die is gain.'

Clearly Paul was not afraid to die for he knew that to be free from the body is to be 'at home with the Lord' (2 Cor. 5:8). Those to whom living means Christ will discover that death only gives us more of Him. For a Christian there is nothing morbid about contemplating what lies beyond death, providing it does not dominate all our thinking. William Grimshaw, mightily used by God in the eighteenth-century revival, pledged as a young man to think of his death every day of his life.

The works of Dostoevesky, the Russian novelist, have such appeal partly because he faced and survived an execution squad. Imminence of death concentrates the mind on what is vital. As the old adage goes: we must deal with death or it will kill us. Paul was a contented and happy man because living meant Christ and dying meant more of Christ. Either way he won.

FURTHER STUDY

Acts 7:55-60;
1 Thess. 4:13-18

1. Why was Stephen's death a victory?

2. What will death mean for a Christian?

Father, I am so thankful that in a world where people are bent on having something to live *with* I have someone to live *for.* I have Jesus in my life. What joy it gives me to know that whether I live or die He remains. Amen.

Self-glorification

FOR READING & MEDITATION - PHILIPPIANS 1:22-26

'I desire to depart and be with Christ, which is better by far; but it is more necessary for you that I remain in the body.' (vv23-24)

In the passage before us now Paul's deliberation about whether to go to be with Jesus or stay sounds as if he is negotiating with God. But that is not so. He is simply weighing up the options. Once again *The Message* puts his thought across with great clarity: 'The desire to break camp here and be with Christ is powerful. Some days I can think of nothing better. But most days, because of what you are going through, I am sure that it's better for me to stick it out here. So I plan to be around awhile, companion to you as your growth and joy in this life of trusting God continues.'

FURTHER STUDY

Isa. 42:8;
1 Cor. 1:18-2:5

1. Who does God choose to use?

2. Why does He choose them?

As Paul contemplates reunion with the Philippians he says: 'through my being with you again your joy in Christ Jesus will overflow on account of me' (v26). The remark could have read: 'through my being with you your joy ... will overflow on account of *me*.' Paul, however, was not a man to leave Jesus out of anything. He could look forward to a great reunion with the Philippians, but the real joy of that reunion would be that together they could celebrate Jesus.

How different to so-called church leaders and evangelists who seek their own glory under the guise of proclaiming Christ. One leader commented: 'I'm not here to show off my clothes but to talk about Jesus.' But of course he did manage to draw attention to his clothes in the way that he chose to introduce Jesus. And not only leaders but many of the laity can be guilty of this same issue – self-glorification. We see tablets on buildings: 'To the glory of God and in memory of _____ who gave a great sum of money for this building.' Sad to say, 'To the glory of God' is far too often an excuse for personal glorification.

God my Father, forgive me if I intrude into the picture and draw attention away from You by my desire for self-glorification. May I know nothing save Jesus Christ and Him crucified. In His peerless name and for His glory I ask it. Amen.

'Divide and destroy'

FOR READING & MEDITATION - PHILIPPIANS 1:27-28

'Whatever happens, conduct yourselves in a manner worthy of
the gospel of Christ.' (v27)

Just as Paul interpreted his circumstances in the light of the gospel (vv13–14) so now he urges the Philippians to make the same gospel the pattern on which to base their lives. Live your lives in such a way, he instructs them, that you are a credit to Christ. What does it mean to live life in such a way that we bring credit to Christ? I believe it means standing firm in one spirit and 'contending as one man for the faith of the gospel' (v27). Paul is giving here a *Christian Charter*.

Disunity in the church is perhaps the most serious impediment to the gospel. If only we would remember we are committed to a common cause like citizens of the same city, athletes playing in the same team, or soldiers fighting on the same side. 'Christian joy and rejoicing,' said George B. Duncan, 'are very closely tied up with human relationships.' The biggest problem in church life is the inability to relate to one another in the spirit of Jesus Christ. It has always been so, is so and will always be so. The thing that so often takes the song from our lips and the joy from our hearts is the fact that we are not living in right relationships with others. Unity and good relationships would make us fearless in the face of any opposition.

FURTHER STUDY

1 Cor. 1:10-17;
Eph. 4:1-7;
Col. 3:12-14

1. What causes disunity?

2. What promotes unity?

Bishop Handley Moule said about the breakup of Christian unity: 'This never happens unless there is sin in the matter, on one side or the other.' He was referring to the sin of resentment, jealousy and so on. Nothing brings more disorder and confusion than disunity. Divide and destroy is Satan's chief strategy. Is there loss of fellowship between you and another Christian? Then put the matter right – today.

Father, help me examine all my relationships and if there is distance between me and others then give me the grace and wisdom to put the matter right without delay. You have spoken to my heart. By Your grace I will obey. In Jesus' name. Amen.

Granted!

FOR READING & MEDITATION – PHILIPPIANS 1:29

'For it has been granted to you on behalf of Christ not only to believe on him, but also to suffer for him' (v29)

Here Paul reminds us that it has been granted to us not only to believe in Jesus but to suffer for Him. One would have thought his statement should read: 'For it is an obligation on behalf of Christ not only to believe on Him but to suffer for Him.' Instead the word 'granted' is used, implying that it is a privilege, an honour to suffer for His sake. John Stott says: 'Suffering is the hallmark of the genuine Church.'

Dietrich Bonhoeffer, the Lutheran pastor who was hanged towards the end of World War II, wrote: 'Discipleship means allegiance to the suffering Christ, and it is therefore not at all surprising that Christians should be called upon to suffer.' But we naturally shrink from the idea of suffering. Here in the West there is very little suffering among Christians. The suffering Paul is referring to in these verses includes not only the suffering that comes from physical persecution but also the harassment and ridicule that can result from taking a stand for Jesus Christ.

FURTHER STUDY

Acts 5:17-42;
2 Tim. 3:12;
1 Pet. 4:12-19

1. What was Peter's response when the apostles were hauled in front of the high priest?

2. Why is suffering a Christian privilege?

Why do modern-day Christians (especially here in the West) not suffer more than they do? We certainly shouldn't court suffering – but we ought not to avoid it either. Perhaps the reason why we do not suffer very much is because our lives do not challenge other lifestyles by their integrity, their purity and their love. The world sees nothing in us that is distinctive. We make little impact on society, we are seldom bold enough to speak out against evil, minding our own business in case anyone should be offended. Faith and suffering are linked together as twin Christian privileges. It is not an obligation to suffer for Jesus. It is a privilege.

God, whenever I am called to suffer for the sake of the gospel give me the insight to see in this an opportunity to be grateful. Together we can turn all adversities into accomplishments. Thank You Father. Amen.

The stimulus of Christ

SAT
19 MAR

FOR READING & MEDITATION – PHILIPPIANS 2:1-4

'make my joy complete by being like-minded, having the same love,
being one in spirit and purpose.' (v2)

The second chapter of Paul's letter to the Philippians opens with his continuing plea for Christian unity. Having encouraged them in the previous chapter to stand firm in one spirit (1:27), he now gives them four further encouragements.

First, that they might *think* alike, to have a mindset that shows common allegiances and loyalties. Second, that they should have not just the same mind but the same love for one another, to share the same feelings and attitudes since their lives have been bound together in common accord. Third, he encourages them to do nothing out of selfish ambition or vain conceit. *The Message* paraphrases this instruction: 'Don't push your way to the front; don't sweet-talk your way to the top. Put yourself aside, and help others get ahead.' Paul's last exhortation in this section is that they should look not to their own interests but to the interests of others.

Is it possible to really live like this – unitedly, lovingly, selflessly, harmoniously? Yes, if we live with and in Jesus. The words 'If you have any encouragement in Christ' (v1) are translated by Moffatt as: 'By all the stimulus of Christ'. Our Lord is not just a Saviour and a Sanctifier, but also a Stimulator – He stimulates us to be what He wants us to be. Notice this emphasis: 'By *all* the stimulus of Christ'. His 'all' is sufficient for our 'all' – and then some. He is the Stimulator of our mind, our emotions and our will. He stimulates our mind to think His thoughts, our feelings to feel as He feels, and our will to do the kind of deeds He would do if He were in our shoes. Open your whole being to His stimulus and you will find that His stimulus, which comes from within, will overcome every stimulus that comes from without.

FURTHER STUDY

John 15:1-17;
2 Cor. 5:14-20

1. How does Jesus stimulate us?

2. What does He stimulate us to do?

Jesus, stimulate my mind to think Your thoughts after You, my feelings to feel Your feelings after You, my will to will Your purposes after You. I open my whole being to Your stimulus now. Help me Lord Jesus. For Your dear name's sake. Amen.

Resourcing Your Church

As well as dated devotional notes, books and training courses, CWR can also support you, your small group and your church through our range of encouraging Church Programmes.

Each of our tried and tested programmes are underpinned by an accompanying book, available to each member of the congregation. These books are designed to encourage and motivate each individual in the church as you journey through the course together.

And the resources do not stop there ... we are committed to supporting your church as fully as possible and so also provide an array of free online materials for you to download and customise, such as sermon outlines, videos, and small group guides. There are now some children's and youth resources available too, so the whole church can follow the same theme at the same time.

Unite your congregation - both faces old and new - by spending a number of weeks learning and worshiping together through one of these church-based initiatives ...

'Going through this resource as a church really inspired us, helping everyone reach a higher level of spirituality and understanding of God's purpose for us.'

40 Days with Jesus by Dave Smith

40 Days with Jesus is a resource that is ideal to commence after Easter, as it follows events and encounters from the resurrection to Jesus' ascension. At its heart is an invitation to actively explore the accounts of the risen Jesus.

Visit **www.40days.info** to find out how your church can draw closer to Jesus.

Transformed Life by Dave Smith

Transformed Life focuses on the first three chapters of Ephesians and looks at answering three of life's key questions: Who am I? Where do I belong? What am I living for?

Visit **www.transformed-life.info** to view resources available for the whole congregation, including young people and those in early and primary years.

Paraclesis by Trevor J. Partridge

Paraclesis (meaning 'to come alongside others') is a fresh approach to pastoral care, developed to engage the whole church family in caring, loving and journeying alongside others in their congregations and wider communities.

Visit **www.paraclesis.info** to discover how you can come alongside your church and community.

Our Lord's outlook

FOR READING & MEDITATION – PHILIPPIANS 2:5
'Your attitude should be the same as that of Christ Jesus' (v5)

Having spoken of the one spirit that binds Christians together, the same love and the need to maintain a spiritual mindset, Paul now turns our attention to the mind of the Master. He alone demonstrates perfectly the mindset that looks not to its own interests. Paul celebrates the example of Jesus in what some scholars consider to have been an early Christian hymn, and urges the Philippians to let the same attitude of mind that was in Jesus to be in them too. Their model (and ours) is nothing less than the incarnation of the eternal Son of God!

FURTHER STUDY

John 10:11-18;
15:13;
1 Cor. 10:23-24

1. How did Jesus demonstrate a selfless mindset?

2. How can we be like Him?

Before we focus on the amazing verses that follow – what one commentator describes as 'the most beautiful Christ-ological passage in the whole of Scripture' – we pause to make note that Paul's *primary* purpose is not to give us a theological exposition of the incarnation but to persuade us that the same mindset that motivated Jesus to leave His home in glory and descend to this sin-cursed planet can be resident in us. It is so easy to get caught up in theological insights that we stop there and fail to apply those insights to daily living. The New King James Version translates the verse before us today like this: 'Let this mind be in you which was also in Christ Jesus.' *The Message* paraphrases it: 'Think of yourselves the way Christ Jesus thought of himself.' And how did Jesus think about Himself? He put the interests of others before His own. He followed the path of selflessness, holding on to nothing as His right. Instead He embarked upon a descending path of ever-increasing service in order that humanity might be saved. This is Jesus' outlook on things. And it can be ours also.

Lord Jesus, give me Your mindset I pray – the mindset that thinks of others more than myself. Forgive me that I am so self-centred and preoccupied with 'me'. I would have Your mind in my mind. Grant it my Saviour. Amen.

'Downward mobility'

FOR READING & MEDITATION – PHILIPPIANS 2:6

'Who, being in very nature God, did not consider equality with God
something to be grasped' (v6)

One of the expressions that has crept into our vocabulary
in the past few decades is the phrase 'upwardly
mobile'. It describes those with a passion for promotion
and advancement; those who strive keenly to get to the top
of the ladder in their profession or vocation. But don't run
away with the idea that upward mobility is a modern-day
phenomenon. Interest in personal promotion dates back to
the Garden of Eden. However, questioning the obsessive
trend towards upward mobility doesn't sit well with many
in contemporary society. Words such as downsizing,
downgrading or demotion push up blood pressures
and send pulses racing.

In the passage before us today we see Jesus
engaging not in upward mobility but downward
mobility. Consider now as Jesus signs up for seven
dramatic demotions; watch as the Son of God
voluntarily descends the ladder into greatness.
Where does He start? At the top. 'Who, being in
very nature God, did not consider equality with
God something to be grasped.' Jesus Christ was
God, remember. Not a created angel, a personal
assistant, a junior partner or vice president. He
was God of very God. The New Revised Standard
Version words it like this: 'He … did not regard
equality with God as something to be exploited.' This is
precisely the point. Jesus did not take advantage of His
exalted position; He did not exploit it for His own selfish
purposes. And when He came among us He did not dazzle
us with displays of overwhelming divine power, nor did He
intimidate us with bullying tactics. He came in humility and
service. Can anything be more amazing?

FURTHER STUDY

Matt. 1:23;
John 1:1-18;
5:18;
1 Tim. 3:16

1. Why did the
Jews want to
kill Jesus?

2. What is the
mystery of
godliness?

**Jesus, each time I dwell on this truth my heart bows in the
deepest worship. How could You ever stoop to descend to my
level? Yet You did. And both now and throughout eternity I will
never cease to praise You. Thank You. Amen.**

More steps down

FOR READING & MEDITATION – PHILIPPIANS 2:7
'but made himself nothing, taking the very nature of a servant,
being made in human likeness.' (v7)

Yesterday we looked at the starting point of our Lord's descent into greatness. He who was God of very God decided for the purposes of redemption to leave His home in glory and live on this sin-stained planet. That was Demotion No. 1. Look now at Demotion No. 2: *but made himself nothing.* Some versions use the phrase 'he emptied himself', which can lead us into asking the question: 'Of what?' The answer that is often supplied is in terms of omnipotence and omniscience. Paul, however, I believe, is not talking of the loss or laying aside of divine attributes but of rendering something powerless, or emptying it of apparent significance. He 'made himself of no reputation' (KJV) is not far short of the mark or, even better, 'he poured himself out'.

FURTHER STUDY

Luke 4:2;
8:23; 22:44;
Gal. 4:4-5

1. List the human experiences of Jesus.

2. Why did God become human?

Demotion No. 3: *taking the very nature of a servant.* The One whom all heaven served became Himself a servant. It seems inconsistent with greatness to see Jesus in such a role as this. In this sin-affected world we think greatness is measured by how many people serve us. Greatness is measured in our celebrity culture by how many know and serve us. But Jesus turns that idea on its head; it's about how many we can serve.

Demotion No. 4: *being made in human likeness.* For Jesus to become a man, wrote the 15th century theologian John Flavel, meant more humiliation than 'for an angel to be turned out of heaven, and be converted into a … worm.' Yet He did not hesitate to do it. And His humanity was real – don't ever forget that. He was not in the guise of a man; He was real man – truly human. Just think of it: the omnipotent God had skin around Him, cribbed, coffined and confined. Is there no length to which our Saviour will not go?

Lord Jesus, it is amazing to ponder the lengths that You went to in order to reach humanity. And behind it all was Your love for lost and helpless people like me. You have my heart. It's Yours for ever. Thank You my Saviour. Amen.

Utterly incredible!

WED
23 MAR

FOR READING & MEDITATION - PHILIPPIANS 2:8

'And being found in appearance as a man, he humbled himself and became obedient to death - even death on a cross!' (v8)

We continue looking at what we are calling the seven dramatic demotions. Demotion No. 5: *And being found in appearance as a man, he humbled himself.* It was not enough that Jesus was found in appearance as a man; his life on earth was a continual selflessness all the way. He allowed people to insult Him, mock Him, say lies about Him and denigrate Him. On more than one occasion onlookers said He was operating under the control of the devil (John 7:20; 8:48)! Imagine that. How did He react? Graciously, lovingly, ungrudgingly. Demotion No. 6: *and became obedient to death.* The Son of God to die? How could God die? How could death strike the Lord of Life? It is the body that dies, not the soul. His body could go down into death but His soul would survive, descend into hell and do battle with Satan, then return in the power of an endless life in a resurrected body.

Demotion No. 7: *even death on a cross!* Are not six demotions enough? Surely to be put to death on a cross was the very basement of debasement. Crucifixion was such a terrible form of execution that it was forbidden for any Roman to die in this way. Yet they put God on a cross. Crucifixion was designed to inflict the maximum amount of pain over the longest possible time.

Earlier we said that the reason Paul wrote these words was not primarily to give us the final and finished formulae on the incarnation, but to call every one of us to live a life of downward mobility. We are in an upside-down kingdom where in order to find we must lose, in order to live we must die, in order to keep we must give away. Jesus lost Himself on purpose, to find you and me. Incredible!

FURTHER STUDY

Isa. 53:1-12;
Heb. 2:9-18;
4:14-5:9

1. Why would people despise Jesus?

2. Why would people admire Him?

Yes, Lord, it's incredible. Utterly incredible. I know of nothing that can move my heart in such a way as the story of Your love. My gratitude knows no bounds. All honour and glory be to Your precious and peerless name. Amen.

A seven-step promotion

FOR READING & MEDITATION - PHILIPPIANS 2:9-11

'Therefore God exalted him to the highest place and gave him the
name that is above every name' (v9)

Over the past three days we have been briefly exploring
the seven dramatic demotions of Jesus. In the section
before us now we see how the sevenfold demotion changes
to a sevenfold promotion. Jesus stepped down from the same
level as the Father to the same level as a thief – from the
highest to the lowest. Now watch the seven-step *promotion*:
(1) *God exalted him to the highest place.* So you see, the
way up is the way down. (2) *gave him the name.* His name
is not just a designation, it is a definition: Saviour. (3) *above
every name.* No name will ever be higher in rank than His.

**FURTHER
STUDY**

2 Tim. 2:11-12;
Rev. 5:1-14

1. What are we
promised if we
'die with Him'?

2. Why is Jesus
worshipped?

(4) *that at the name of Jesus every knee should
bow.* Maybe not now but one day every person will.
(5) *in heaven and on earth and under the earth.*
His rule will be universal. (6) *and every tongue
confess that Jesus Christ is Lord.* People may not
wish to acknowledge His Lordship but they will
have to recognise it. (7) *to the glory of God the
Father.* Ultimately God will be glorified in His
universe and no one will be able to prevent this.
The mind that was in Jesus lost itself in the deepest
renunciation possible and found itself in the highest
annunciation possible. Jesus Christ is *Lord.*

What does all of this say to us? That self-realisation is
found by self-renunciation. In His mind Jesus set no limit as
to the amount of service that He was prepared to undergo.
Jesus never said to the Father: 'I will go so far and no further.'
He could not have gone any further than He went. Can such
a mind be found in us? Not unless we live close to Jesus,
assimilate His spirit and absorb His attitudes. When we are
prepared to go down with Him then we go up with Him.

**Jesus, I see so clearly that when I am identified with You in self-
surrender and obedience I am identified with a name that is above
every other name. Of what consequence is my name when I can
have Yours! Thank You dear Saviour. Amen.**

Attention: God at work

FOR READING & MEDITATION – PHILIPPIANS 2:12-13

'Therefore, my dear friends ... continue to work out your salvation
with fear and trembling, for it is God who works in you' (vv12-13)

The stunning picture of Jesus that Paul has just painted in
verses 6 to 11 comes with a 'therefore' attached, calling us
to respond. Someone has commented that whenever you see
the word 'therefore' in the Scriptures you must ask yourself:
'What it is there for?' So what is Paul saying to us here? This:
just as Jesus kept on doing what the Father asked Him to do,
so we must do the same. In other words, we must continue
to live in responsive obedience to the divine commands.

The instruction 'work out your own salvation' is not, as
some suppose, a reference to salvation by works. We are
not working to be saved; we are working because
we are saved. The thought here is not so much that
we should work out the salvation God has given
us from within but work it out to its completion;
live out the life we possess in Jesus. This Good
Friday let us remind ourselves that passivity in
the Christian life is not an option; a 'let go and let
God' attitude will not do. We learn to co-operate
with the strength and energy of God working in
us. Deep within the springs of each Christian's
personality God is at work redirecting our wills
and rejuvenating our motivation to do His will!
This is the glorious reality of the new covenant life once
promised by Jeremiah and made good by the Holy Spirit
(Ezek. 36:26).

**FURTHER
STUDY**

Eph. 2:1-10;
2 Pet. 1:1-11

1. For what
has God
prepared us?

2. What can
we add to
our faith?

Next time you catch yourself saying, 'I can't do God's will,
I'm too weak, I keep failing,' let God's Word reverberate
within your soul. He says: 'I am working actively inside you
to will and to bring about what pleases Me. I am continuing
the good work I began in you and will bring it to completion.'
How awesome! God is at work in us.

**God, I see clearly that a divine strategy is at work. I am part of
a purpose that will go on through all the days of my life until I
meet with You in eternity. You will never fail me; may I never fail
You. For Jesus' sake I ask it. Amen.**

'Holes in the darkness'

FOR READING & MEDITATION - PHILIPPIANS 2:14-16

'Do everything without complaining or arguing, so that you may become blameless and pure' (vv14-15)

*T*he *Message* paraphrases Paul's opening words here in this way: 'Do everything readily and cheerfully – no bickering, no second-guessing allowed! Go out into the world uncorrupted, a breath of fresh air in this squalid and polluted society.' The NIV tells us that when we carry the light of Jesus into the darkness of the world's night we shine 'like stars in the universe'. We live in a world where celebrities are famous merely for being famous. But there are no stars in that sense in God's earthly firmament. To be a star in God's eyes demands no heroic exploits – only the major feat of not grumbling or complaining!

FURTHER STUDY

Isa. 60:1-3;
Matt. 5:13-16;
2 Cor. 4:1-6;
Eph. 5:8-9

1. What are the works and words of light?

2. What is the fruit of light?

Paul bears down again on the need for true authentic living. It's an issue that is so important he has to return to it again and again. And it's the same in our day too. How many Christian communities would be transformed if people stopped grizzling and griping and disputing among themselves? Nothing brings Christians to a dead halt more quickly than their inability to get along with one another. Even more serious, I believe, is to grumble and grizzle in front of those with no faith for this, as Oswald Chambers writes, is to cast a slur on the reputation of God! As disciples and followers of Jesus we need to take care to shine in the darkness, not add to the blackness by our unChristian attitudes.

Robert Louis Stevenson, one evening, stood transfixed at his nursery window watching the lamplighter in the street. When his nanny asked the boy what he was doing he replied: 'I'm watching the man knocking holes in the darkness.' We live in a universe made dark by sin. Let's knock holes in the darkness.

Gracious Father, I long to shine as a star in *Your* eyes. Keep me true to You in all things so that I, like Paul, might hold out the word of life in a crooked and depraved generation. Help me to knock some holes in the darkness. Amen.

'There is another world'

FOR READING & MEDITATION – PHILIPPIANS 2:17-18

'But even if I am being poured out like a drink offering on the sacrifice and service coming from your faith, I am glad' (v17)

Once more we come to Easter Sunday – the most glorious day on the Christian calendar. One person has pointed out that the word Easter, when taken as an acrostic, can spell out: Every Alternative Saviour Takes Early Retirement. Our Saviour will never take retirement; He lives and is active for ever. Indeed He poured Himself out for us – both in life and death.

The imagery used here of being 'poured out like a drink offering' was no doubt a reference to the outpouring of wine that accompanied the burnt offerings and grain offerings made daily in first the tabernacle and then the Temple. Paul acknowledges that his ministry exhausts his energies and entails suffering. But this 'sacrifice' is not dragged from him reluctantly; it is part of his willing and joyful self-offering in the cause of the gospel. Even more remarkably, he turns matters on their head by telling the Philippians that his outpouring of life is a drink offering that climaxes *their* sacrifice, not his! They can therefore rejoice in each other's plight!

Isn't it extraordinary that the self-offering of apostles and martyrs is the crowning seal of value placed on our faith? Of Bishop Ryle it was said that he woke each morning and thought of his bed as an altar, so dedicating himself as a living sacrifice to God each day. John Wesley was a classical scholar with a huge love of books, yet he spent most of his life in the saddle. He sacrificed those things in order to blow the trumpet for Jesus Christ. 'I have a relish for books,' he said, 'but there is another world.' There is. Thank Jesus today for His sacrifice, which has opened the way for us to sacrifice ourselves to His incredible purposes.

FURTHER STUDY

John 17:13-18; 18:36; Rom. 12:1-2

1. How can we be in the world but not of it?

2. What sacrifices do we offer God?

Father, I must ask myself today: How much do I sacrifice for the sake of the gospel? How much of what I do is done for that other world? Help me get all my perspectives straight and may I always give eternity the casting vote. Amen.

Hope ... in the Lord Jesus

FOR READING & MEDITATION - PHILIPPIANS 2:19

'I hope in the Lord Jesus to send Timothy to you soon, that I also may be cheered when I receive news about you.' (v19)

How interesting that when Paul says he hopes to send Timothy to see the Philippians he uses the phrase 'I hope *in the Lord Jesus*.' There is a great difference between hope and hope *in the Lord Jesus*. Hope, says one New Testament scholar, was a word that the inhabitants of the ancient world distrusted. In today's world also there are those who have no room for hope in their approach to life. But, for Christians, hope in the Lord Jesus has been found to be a true hope that *can* be trusted. Jesus Himself, while standing in the shadow of the cross, said 'take heart! I have overcome the world' (John 16:33).

FURTHER STUDY

Acts 4:18-25;
15:4;
Heb. 6:13-20

1. How do we obtain and develop hope?

2. How does hope keep us firm and secure?

Throughout his writings, Paul spends a lot of time talking about hope. Take these verses, for example: 'May the God of hope fill you with all joy and peace as you trust in him, so that you may overflow with hope by the power of the Holy Spirit' (Rom. 15:13). 'And now these three remain: faith, hope and love' (1 Cor. 13:13). 'Not only so, but we also rejoice in our sufferings, because we know that suffering produces perseverance; perseverance, character; and character, hope. And hope does not disappoint us, because God has poured out his love into our hearts by the Holy Spirit, whom he has given us' (Rom. 5:3-5).

Paul's focus on hope 'in the Lord Jesus' was not mere wishful thinking, but a hope that was solid and concrete. He knew, for example, that Timothy's visit would bring joy to the Philippians and later to himself when Timothy returned with news about them. Hoping 'in the Lord Jesus' meant that he knew good would come of that visit. Remind yourself this Easter season that good comes of everything when we hope in Him.

Loving Lord Jesus, help me this day and every day to live in Your victory and hope in Your hope, just as Paul did. For Your own dear name's sake. Amen.

The real thing

FOR READING & MEDITATION – PHILIPPIANS 2:20-24

'I have no-one else like him, who takes a genuine interest in
your welfare.' (v20)

In this passage Paul gives a glowing testimony to his son in
the faith, Timothy. 'I have no-one else like him,' he says.
An enthusiastic tribute indeed. Having written earlier of the
importance of selflessness he makes the point that Timothy
illustrates this better than anyone else in his immediate circle.
He 'takes a genuine interest in your welfare' is his summary
of this choice disciple. 'Most people around here,' adds Paul,
'are looking out for themselves, with little concern for the
things of Jesus. But ... Timothy's the real thing' (*The Message*).

Permit me to ask a personal question: Are you the kind
of person who takes a genuine interest in the
affairs of others? One of the reasons why God has
put you in the church or group in which you now
find yourself is to be genuinely concerned about
others. Dr E. Stanley Jones said: 'Life is sensitivity.
The lowest life is sensitive only to itself. The higher
in the scale of existence you come, the wider the
range of sensitivity and the deeper the depth ... You
can tell how far you have risen in the scale of life
by asking one question: How widely do I care and
how deeply?'

After his commendation of Timothy, Paul
concludes this section by again using the phrase *in
the Lord.* 'I am confident *in the Lord,*' he says, 'that I myself
will come soon.' Because Paul was confident *in the Lord* he
subjected his wishes and desires to divine approval. 'In the
Lord' gives a new dimension to everything, for if we have
confidence in Him then we do not bargain with Him; we will
trust His goodness and His love. He will give us the thing
hoped for, or something different – something closer to His
purposes than our own.

FURTHER STUDY

Jer. 22:15-16;
Acts 9:36-42

1. What is
the result
of knowing
the Lord?

2. How was
Dorcas' faith
the real thing?

**Father, teach me how to submit all my wishes and desires to Your
wishes and desires. May I approach life with the confidence that
You know best in everything. And You always give the best to
those who leave the final choice to You. Amen.**

It matters

FOR READING & MEDITATION - PHILIPPIANS 2:25-28

'But I think it is necessary to send back to you Epaphroditus,
my brother, fellow-worker and fellow-soldier' (v25)

Yesterday we saw that concern for others was one of
Timothy's chief characteristics. The same can be said of
Epaphroditus. Another devoted servant of God, Epaphroditus
is described by Paul as a 'fellow-worker and fellow-soldier'
who had 'almost died for the work of Christ' (v30). Clearly
Epaphroditus also was high on the scale of caring!

In Timothy and Epaphroditus we see the qualities of
unselfish concern and unstinted service. The physical
effort and exhaustion, the illness that dogged Epaphroditus'
footsteps as he worked himself to his limits in serving
the Philippians, put his life in danger. What
outstanding servants these two men were. It is
interesting that some of Jesus' apostles rate only
half a line of Scripture while these two 'ordinary'
workers rate half a chapter! Equally heart-warming
is the reminder that Paul was no lone-wolf but a
person who gathered men around him who were
friends, not functionaries.

FURTHER STUDY

1 Cor. 16:14-20;
Col. 4:7-18

1. What are
the qualities
of 'unsung
heroes'?

2. How did
Paul show
that people
mattered
to him?

Timothy and Epahroditus are two of the gospel's
countless 'unsung heroes'. Timothy was a role
model in seeking the interests of others rather
than his own, and was as near to a son as Paul ever
had. Epaphroditus was evidently missing home and
worrying how the Philippians might be reacting to
news of his illness. How very human! 'Welcome
him back,' says Paul, 'without thinking he has let you down
by returning when in fact he risked his neck for me.'

All in all this is a wonderful illustration of how redemption
transfigures everyday events, and the Holy Spirit inspires
a practical down-to-earth spirituality. Who you are, what
you are doing and even where you are going today matters
to the Lord. It really does.

**Father, may these two qualities - unselfish concern and unstinted
service - be found in me as I live out my life. Physical danger
may not be a threat but my service offered is to be self-sacrificial
nevertheless. Help me my Father. Amen.**

'You're not home yet'

FOR READING & MEDITATION – PHILIPPIANS 2:29-30

'Welcome him in the Lord with great joy, and honour men like him'
(v29)

Paul's wish for Epaphroditus is that when he returns to the congregation in Philippi the Christians there will receive him *in the Lord with great joy*. Notice the use of the phrase 'in the Lord' once again. *The Message* says: 'Give him a grand welcome, a joyful embrace!' How sad that so many of God's servants who have given themselves in service are taken for granted rather than greeted with gratitude.

A missionary tells how he came back to his home church after serving on the mission field for thirty years and did not even hear his name mentioned until several weeks after he had returned. Other churches in his area invited him to speak to them about his missionary endeavours, but his own church seemed to ignore him. How disappointing. The missionary concerned, a fine and godly man, was not looking for applauds, but it hurt him nevertheless when his work for God went unrecognised by his home church. When writing about this situation later he admitted: 'One night, when feeling lonely and unappreciated, I wept before the Lord and cried out to Him saying: "Lord, I came home and no one even gave me a word of appreciation or thanks. Is this really what a homecoming is like?"' He went on to record how God drew very close to him and filled his heart with the most wonderful sense of consolation and love and whispered to him: 'Don't worry, you're not home yet.'

One day that missionary will arrive home and hear from the lips of God Himself the words 'Well done.' It's sad, though, that some of God's faithful servants have to wait until they reach heaven to be honoured. Such servants deserve honour here on earth as well.

FURTHER STUDY

Matt. 8:5-13;
25:14-29;
1 Thess. 5:12-13

1. What is God's attitude to faithful servants?

2. What should be our attitude?

My Father and my God, build in me a true appreciation of those whose lives show such unselfish concern and unstinted service, and help me to honour them as they deserve to be honoured. In Jesus' name I pray.

All Over the World

Jesus is worshipped, the Bible is read and the gospel is preached in more languages and more places than any other religion worldwide.

We are living in an era where Christianity is a world religion, with the majority of believers now living in Africa, Asia and Latin America.

CWR's ministry, whilst primarily based in the UK, reaches far and wide, and we are honoured to be called to serve the Church outside of our 'four walls'.

Asia

God has opened doors for our teaching, training and printed resources to reach thousands in Singapore and Malaysia, rippling across South East Asia. We are currently working with the church in Cambodia to bring our counselling training to the region, and several of our publications are being translated into Sinhala, Tamil, Mandarin and Korean. New opportunities are arising so regularly, that we covet your prayers and support for wisdom and funding to enable us to follow and provide where God is leading.

Africa

Our training and publications – particularly *Every Day with Jesus* – are welcomed and devoured across many African nations including Nigeria, Ghana, Kenya, Uganda and South Africa. Whether shipped from the UK or printed locally, our resources are reaching homes, churches and prisons across the continent, thanks to your support, prayers and generous donations.

Australasia

From all regions of Australia and New Zealand, we frequently receive testimonies of how our teaching, Bible reading notes, books and DVDs are helping build and disciple God's people.

A ministry serving those in prison and those released recently contacted us:

> 'Thank you. The resources you supply have been a huge blessing as we are always on the alert for books and DVDs that assist progressive rehabilitation and reintegration by the Christian Way.'

If you would like to support our ministry around the world, we would value:

- Your prayer for wisdom and favour to continue to minister in areas where God has made a way for us
- Your support in making our resources and training known in your region
- Your generosity in helping us fund this vital provision for our brothers and sisters, and in growing and developing our ministry into these existing and new regions

If you would like to make a donation, please fill in the 'Gift to CWR' section on the order form at the back of this publication, completing the Gift Aid declaration if appropriate.

'Danger: savage dogs'

FOR READING & MEDITATION - PHILIPPIANS 3:1-2
'Finally, my brothers, rejoice in the Lord!' (v1)

This third chapter of Paul's 'epistle of joy' has a strong personal note running through it. Paul begins and ends by referring to those who have different views from his own, but the core of the chapter deals with his personal spiritual experience.

The word 'finally' in the opening verse of the chapter sounds slightly incongruous when you consider he is far from finishing his letter. However, it does not indicate that Paul is uncertain when to finish, but should be taken in the sense of 'above all, rejoice', or 'in the end, rejoice'. In every issue he dealt with Paul wanted joy to be his final note.

FURTHER STUDY

Gal. 3:1-14;
4:17;
5:1-6;
6:12-13

1. Why were preachers of circumcision so dangerous?

2. What were their motives?

In the next verse (v2) some serious name calling goes on: 'Watch out there are dogs about!' Who is this fierce talk aimed at and why? As with the Galatians, it seems the Philippians were being troubled by some Jewish Christians who wanted to impose on Gentile believers the specific marks of Jewishness – particularly circumcision. From the time of Abraham onwards, circumcision was the outward sign in males of being in God's covenant family. This was especially important for Jews living outside the Promised Land, and was a contentious issue in the apostolic mission.

Circumcision, though, was always meant to signify a deeper 'circumcision of the heart', accomplished by God Himself (see Deut. 30:6). What is more, since Jesus has come, circumcision no longer counts for anything in a disciple's relationship with God. As far as Paul was concerned, to say otherwise was to threaten the freedom of the gospel of grace. Understandably, then, Paul does not mince his words. You have to be strong when the truth is at stake.

God, help me to be strong, too, when truth is being challenged, especially Your truth. Give me an even deeper realisation of how precious my freedom in Jesus is. I am so glad my faith does not have to be supplemented by special rites. Amen.

Nothing else

FOR READING & MEDITATION – PHILIPPIANS 3:3

'For it is we who are the circumcision, we who worship by the Spirit of God, who glory in Christ Jesus' (v3)

Yesterday we noted that for Paul faith in Jesus was the only essential sign of belonging to God's covenant family. He reacted with an appropriate strength of feeling to anyone who claimed that Jesus is not enough for salvation. We too can have that confidence.

In the verse before us now Paul celebrates the fact that the Philippian Christians – both Jewish and Gentile – are bona fide members of God's new covenant community. Physical circumcision, operative from Abraham's day, is now obsolete and the real 'circumcised ones' can be defined as those who enjoy the privileges of the new covenant relationship promised by the prophets long ago. We serve or 'worship by the Spirit of God'. To live 'in the flesh' is to live centred on oneself and without God; to live 'by the Spirit' is to live a human life in all its aspects guided, strengthened and energised by the Spirit of God.

Furthermore, our worship is characterised by the way we 'glory in Christ Jesus'. Trusting Jesus and experiencing the Spirit are the only authentic signs of our being in God's covenant family. Our trademark is that we put away any confidence in our own abilities but recognise our dependence on Him. As Paul argues, our status before God and our relationship with Him do not depend on any inherited patterns of privilege or achievements of our own piety, but solely on Jesus and the Spirit. We are in God's covenant family through grace.

Jesus had saved Paul from leaning on any prop to bolster his faith. Faith and life were reduced to simplicity. Jesus Christ *alone* was and is the centre of his glorying. That's something to sing about isn't it?

FURTHER STUDY

Gal. 4:21-31; 5:16-18; 6:14-16

1. What is the result of living in the flesh?

2. What is the result of living in the Spirit?

Lord Jesus Christ, as I meditate on Your surpassing worth I see that everything else is superfluous. I can say 'No' to every rite and ceremony because I have said 'Yes' to You. Since I have You for ever I need nothing and no one else. Amen.

Impeccable pedigree

FOR READING & MEDITATION - PHILIPPIANS 3:4-9

'But whatever was to my profit I now consider loss for the sake of Christ.' (v7)

Paul now rehearses his impeccable pedigree as a member of God's people, the Israelites. There are some who believe that Paul rejected his past, but that is not so. The apostle was always conscious of the high honour of his Jewish heritage. Here and elsewhere in his writings we learn that he loved the patriarchs, honoured the law, worshipped at the Temple and synagogue and soaked himself in the Hebrew Scriptures. He never denigrated these things in themselves, only the *false confidence* he had once placed in them.

FURTHER STUDY

Rom. 9:1-5,16;
10:1-13;
Gal. 3:19-25

1. Why was Paul's pedigree inadequate for salvation?

2. How did he know God before and after his conversion?

In one sense there was nothing wrong with Paul's past except that there was no future in it! Apart from Jesus he could never by keeping the law have experienced deep inner peace. The law, as he told the Galatians, was his schoolmaster to bring him to Jesus (see Gal. 3:24, KJV). Sadly, zeal for the law led him to persecute the Church. In other respects, though, he could claim to be 'blameless' as far as the righteousness of the law was concerned. In saying this, Paul was not claiming to have been faultless, but he could be seen to be without blame because he had kept to the letter of the law - when he sinned he made recompense in the way the law instructed. But his law-keeping had become distorted into his own righteousness (v9). Though appreciative of his heritage, he was willing to count it as loss because of 'the surpassing greatness of knowing Christ Jesus my Lord' (v8).

Notice the word 'knowing' in the phrase in verse 8; it means far more than knowing about Him or knowing a system built up around Him – it means knowing Him personally, closely, intimately. Do you know Him like that? If not, you can this very day.

Lord Jesus, is it any wonder that when people find You they regard everything they had depended upon for salvation - good works, self-effort, self-sacrifice - as nothing? In You is fullness, everything else is emptiness. Thank You. Amen.

'Revised balance sheet'

FOR READING & MEDITATION – PHILIPPIANS 3:5-11

'What is more, I consider everything a loss compared to the
surpassing greatness of knowing Christ Jesus my Lord' (v8)

In this rich and famous passage (vv5–11) Paul dwells on
several points. First, like an accountant examining his
spiritual assets, Paul draws up his accounts. In what has
been called Paul's 'revised balance-sheet' the apostle reveals
(as we saw yesterday) that his old status and privileges did
not, in any way, amount to the joys of salvation in Jesus.
In fact, all that was previously profitable to him he had
decisively written off, consigning it to the shredder! This
is tough talk from Paul, especially about things that were
once so important and precious to him. But knowing Jesus
surpasses everything else. As we discovered
yesterday, knowing Jesus involves much more
than knowing about Him or belonging to a religious
system linked to Him. It means knowing Him
personally. Only this kind of relationship really
transforms our lives.

FURTHER STUDY

Gal. 3:26-4:7;
Col. 2:13-14

1. What was
the balance
against us?

2. What is the
balance for us?

Second, it is worth noting how closely Paul's
testimony mirrors the summary of Jesus' life in
2:5–11. Like his Lord, Paul renounced a privileged
status, suffered loss, underwent humiliation and
gave up his life for the cause of the gospel.

Third, if we were to ask Paul 'Was it worth it?' he would
surely reply with a resounding 'Yes!' He had gained a
relationship with Jesus and knew that in the future he
was sure he would be 'found in Christ', with covenant
membership not guaranteed by the law, right of birth, a
particular upbringing, ritual or anything else but given by
God to those who believe in Jesus. 'Found in him' (v9) – what
a marvellous phrase. What this passage makes incredibly
clear is that Paul wanted to be found in Christ – not in
anything else.

**Father, once again I rejoice that I have found this same simplicity
of faith and life and love as the apostle Paul. Save me from all
that saps my energy, my love and my loyalty. I would have a
single-minded devotion to You and You alone. Amen.**

The School of Calvary

FOR READING & MEDITATION - PHILIPPIANS 3:10-11

'I want to know Christ and the power of his resurrection ...
becoming like him in his death' (v10)

The extraordinary re-evaluation of his life that Paul had undergone gave him a completely new ambition: he declares that he wants above all to know Jesus and the power of His resurrection. But Paul already knew Him. So what did he mean? Surely he meant that whatever he knew of Him there was still much more to be known. In other words, he wants to know Him more and more. Isn't that the desire of us all?

For Paul, knowing Jesus *more* involved entering into a deeper experience both of His risen power and His suffering

FURTHER STUDY

Acts 26:9-29; Eph. 3:14-19

1. How was Paul a graduate of the School of Calvary?

2. How can knowing surpass knowledge?

death! It was not a dead Jew he wanted to know but a living, resurrected and universal Saviour. Paul looked back on the experience of knowing Jesus as being definitely worth the price. He might have written in his personal journal: 'I died on the Damascus Road. My previous life bit the dust and all my intellectual and moral achievements vanished when I had that breathtaking encounter with Jesus, crucified and risen.'

So when Paul speaks of knowing Jesus more he is speaking out of an already profound, firsthand experience – of knowing Jesus penetrating to the depths of his personality, of Jesus being the dominating influence in his life, of Jesus giving him the surge of courage to face an angry mob, of Jesus turning the moral effort of a legalistic past into a life-stretching adventure with the Holy Spirit, of Jesus filling the wings of his abilities and ambitions. And knowing all that he says he still wants to know Him! Having been enrolled in the curriculum of Jesus' sufferings, Paul is willing, for the further joy set before him, to become a graduate of the 'School of Calvary' whatever it cost. Are you?

Resurrected and living Lord, I too would know You and the power of Your resurrection in every thought, every word, every attitude, every moment of the day and night. I am grateful for what I already know of You but I long to know more. Amen.

'That's the gospel'

FOR READING & MEDITATION - PHILIPPIANS 3:10-11

'I want to know Christ and the power of his resurrection and the fellowship of sharing in his sufferings' (v10)

So important are these verses that we spend another day considering them. *I want to know ... the fellowship of sharing in his sufferings.* What can this mean?

It means holding shares in Jesus' sufferings. The resurrection did not cancel out the cross, so that Jesus did all the dying, while we do all the triumphing. No! By raising Jesus from the dead God endorsed the whole self-giving, servant lifestyle that had taken Him to the cross. So, if we enjoy the power of his resurrection working in us – and by the Spirit we certainly do – then we must realise it is intended to empower us to enter into the fellowship of His sufferings in the real world, to carry the pain of rejection as He carried it, to bear scorn as He bore it. Nothing could be more relevant to today's Church, especially those over-triumphalist sections that want the glory but may not necessarily be prepared to accept the cross.

The second phrase we consider is found in verse 11 in which Paul talks about attaining 'to the resurrection from the dead'. Paul's great anticipation – and indeed that of everyone who believes that Jesus rose from the dead – was resurrection. He knew that the statistics concerning death are impressive – one out of every one dies. But his confidence was in the fact that through death he would eventually come out on to the other side into life – endless life. Resurrection is the way God ultimately restores His people and demonstrates that they are really His. The whole message of verses 5–11 can be summed up like this: the way of the cross leads home, the way of death leads to life and the way down is the way up. That's the gospel.

FURTHER STUDY

2 Cor. 4:7-18;
Gal. 2:20;
2 Tim. 2:8-10

1. How does the way of death lead to life?

2. How did Paul know 'the fellowship of his sufferings'?

Father, I am so grateful that though death may separate my body from my soul, You have plans for a new body to be united to my soul – a body like Your glorious body. How amazing! Thank You Father. Amen.

'Full stretch for Him'

FOR READING & MEDITATION - PHILIPPIANS 3:12-14

'I press on to take hold of that for which Christ Jesus took hold of me.' (v12)

As we said earlier, this third chapter is centred around the intimacy that comes through continued communion with Jesus. And no one in the long history of the Church has lived more closely to Jesus than the apostle Paul. He goes on now to give us some vivid and revealing insights into his own spiritual progress.

Using the metaphor of a race, Paul makes two virtually parallel statements in which the central message, emphasised twice, is: *I press on* (vv12,14). Paul brackets this intense sense of purpose with three disclaimers, which give a realistic

FURTHER STUDY

Psa. 84:1-12;
Acts 20:22-24;
21:13

1. What desires did the psalmist express?

2. How did Paul's desires translate into actions?

context for his aspirations. He has not yet obtained his spiritual goal, not yet been made perfect and does not consider himself to have taken hold of his final destiny. Paul is under no illusions about the present life. He has gained life in Jesus but is aware there is so much more for him to know and receive in God's well-stocked future. His eye is on that future as a goal to be reached.

Recalling how he was apprehended by Jesus on the Damascus Road, Paul now presses on to take hold of that for which Jesus took hold of him. On the Damascus Road Paul's career was turned completely around. Now Jesus' agenda is all-important to Paul; God's purposes, not Paul's plans, matter most.

The goal and the prize that await at the finishing tape – whatever way you look at them – can only be that ultimate experience of knowing Jesus – which Paul has already told us is his over-riding ambition. What a wonderful day this would be for all of us if we took a few moments to rededicate our lives to Jesus and determine no matter what from now on we will live out our lives at 'full stretch' for Him.

God, You are all I want, but I want more of what I want. I yield myself afresh to You today. Help me to be at 'full stretch' for You in everything I do this day and every day. For Jesus' sake. Amen.

Focused living

FOR READING & MEDITATION - PHILIPPIANS 3:13-14

'But one thing I do' (v13)

W e pause to reflect further on Paul's powerful testimony concerning his own spiritual desire by focusing on the phrase 'one thing I do'. If we are to make spiritual progress our relationship with Jesus becomes our priority and we concentrate on the 'one thing needed' (see Luke 10:42). Søren Kierkegaard, the enigmatic but prophetic nineteenth-century Dane, titled one of his books, *Purity of Heart is to Will One Thing*. Dissipation of energy gets us nowhere in the spiritual walk. If we spread ourselves too thinly we cover very little. We are followers of Him who was the most focused man in all history.

American pastor Washington Gladden once said, 'It is better to say, "This one thing I do" than to say, "These forty things I dabble in".' But this need not be so. We can ask God to help us regroup our scattered resources or, where appropriate, streamline our commitments. It is perfectly possible to become single-minded without being narrow-minded. Kierkegaard introduced the aforementioned book by praying that God would give 'to the intellect, wisdom to comprehend that one thing; to the heart, sincerity to receive this understanding; to the will, purity that wills only one thing ... amid distractions, collectedness to will one thing; in suffering, patience to will one thing.'

Management consultants and efficiency experts say it all the time: 'Do fewer things and do them better.' Go over your life in God's presence and ask yourself: Am I over-committed? Ought I to pull back from doing some of the good things I am involved in so that I might concentrate on giving myself to the best? Better to say 'One thing I do' than 'These many things I dabble in.'

FURTHER STUDY

Matt. 6:33;
Luke 10:38-42;
14:16-24

1. What things can clutter our lives?

2. What one thing should we do?

Father, if my life is cluttered with good things that prevent me from giving my attention to the best, then help me simplify the clutter by taking to heart Paul's words today. In Jesus' name. Amen.

Past landmarks

FOR READING & MEDITATION – PHILIPPIANS 3:13

'Forgetting what is behind and straining towards what is ahead,
I press on' (vv13-14)

We should perhaps not put too heavy a psychological interpretation on Paul's statement, 'Forgetting what is behind,' though this is often done in sermons and in seminars. It's certainly true that we need not linger on regrets or memories or failures or limited education or hindrances of life to stop us pressing forward with Jesus. But it is unlikely that Paul is referring either to previous deprivations or even to his pre-Christian past, which he has recently rehearsed. When Paul uses the athletic imagery elsewhere it is usually with reference to his apostolic ministry. So the likely point at issue here is Paul's refusal to rest on past successes in his determination to press on towards the goal. He wants to do this without distractions. We need to keep the race metaphor simple. Whatever else you do, don't look back. 'Keep on keeping on' was a motto popular with Christians in the first half of the twentieth century.

FURTHER STUDY

1 Cor. 9:24-27;
Gal. 5:7-10;
Heb. 12:1-3

1. What can hinder us in the Christian race?

2. What helps us?

Sporting enthusiasts of a certain age will never forget that memorable mile race at the Empire Games held in Vancouver in August 1954 when John Landy, the Australian champion, looked back over his left shoulder to see where Roger Bannister was, only to have Bannister pass him on his right!

J.B. Lightfoot, a great nineteenth-century scholar, paraphrased Paul's words in this way: 'Do not mistake me, I hold the language of hope, not of assurance ... forgetting the landmarks already passed and straining every nerve and muscle in the onward race, I press forward toward the goal.' Landmarks tell you where you are and where you have come from. Signposts point to the way ahead. Don't dawdle at the landmarks; follow the signposts.

Father, I accept the challenge of focusing more on signposts than on landmarks. Forgive me if I prefer to look back to the past rather than ahead to the future. Lead me on, Father. Ever on. In Jesus' name. Amen.

'A jubilant pining'

FOR READING & MEDITATION – PHILIPPIANS 3:15

'All of us who are mature should take such a view of things.' (v15)

Paul now encourages the Philippian converts to be mature by sharing the 'view of things' he has just described. Based on Paul's example and the passage that we have been looking at, there are at least six characteristics of a person who has a mature view of things.

(1) *An unwavering commitment to knowing Jesus Christ.* Douglas Webster, a Christian commentator, has said: 'Knowing Jesus involves a personal encounter, an exclusive relationship, a permanent union, and a transformed life.' That's enough for two lifetimes! (2) *A realistic appraisal of our own progress.* 'Not that I have already obtained all this' (v12). Discerning the New Testament's creative tension between what we have now and what we hope for but do not yet have is the beginning of spiritual wisdom. (3) *An unsentimental attitude to the past.* We learn to forget, not by failing to recall God's mercies however they have come, but in the sense of not being paralysed by the memory of failures or nostalgia for past securities.

(4) *An undiminished desire for God* – what the hymn writer H.W. Faber called 'a jubilant pining and longing for God'. (5) *An undistracted focus on the things that really matter so that we do fewer things better.* And (6) *an unabashed tendency to be forward looking.* Paul's eyes were always on the coming day and coming Saviour, on the end, the prize, the goal. He was not anchored to the past, but drawn irresistibly onwards by the magnet of God's future.

Reflect now on these six characteristics at the same time asking yourself: How mature am I? If you are like me you will probably say: 'There's room for improvement.' But press on; don't stop now.

FURTHER STUDY

Eph. 4:11-16;
2 Pet. 3:18

1. What are the marks of a mature Christian?

2. What are the marks of immaturity?

Father, may I become a more mature person. Help me to see that spiritual development is not so much my responsibility as my response to Your ability. Enable me to grow. In Jesus' name. Amen.

Keep on track

FOR READING & MEDITATION – PHILIPPIANS 3:15-16

'Only let us live up to what we have already attained.' (v16)

Eugene Peterson paraphrases Paul's words here in this way: 'Now that we're on the right track, let's stay on it.' It's sad how many Christians get off track in the Christian life. Once in London, a group of men who had trained together for the Christian ministry thirty-five years earlier met for a reunion. One of these men commented afterwards: 'The group could easily be divided into two categories: the world-weary, resigned and virtually retired, and those who have retained their energy and eagerness for new adventures, their keen sense of calling.' If this happens with men who occupy the pulpit, what about those who sit in the congregation?

FURTHER STUDY

Eph. 4:17-32;
Col. 3:5-12;
1 John 3:16

1. How do we put off the old self?

2. How do we put on the new self?

Even in the best churches we will inevitably meet varied levels of spiritual maturity. Mature Christians will handle this situation without disparaging or patronising those not as 'far down the track'. Paul's advice is to trust God to open everyone's eyes so that they will see things from the same point of view (v15). God can bring everyone 'up to speed', as it were, so that the progress of the many is not dragged back by the slowest member. In an atmosphere of mutual respect there is room for a growing understanding on many issues, though some issues, of course, are non-negotiable – the crucified life, for example, or the enthusiastic pursuit of the call of God.

The bottom line is simple: 'Live in accordance with the light you have received.' That is all we can expect of anyone. However, since what we have received in Jesus is so life-changing, none need become apathetic or complacent. As Duncan Campbell once urged: let's not 'settle for anything less than heaven wills to give us'. Indeed.

Jesus, You are adequacy and You are power. So I come again to You for adequacy and power to live by. Once more I throw open every part of my being to Your challenge. Help me not to settle for anything less than heaven wills to give. Amen.

He died climbing!

FOR READING & MEDITATION - PHILIPPIANS 3:17

'Join with others in following my example, brothers, and take note of those who live according to the pattern we gave you.' (v17)

At first, the idea of following Paul's example sounds as daunting as it does attractive. His instruction could be paraphrased: 'Imitate me as I imitate Christ.' How is it possible for anyone to imitate the great apostle? When Paul issued the challenge to imitate him, however, he did not expect this to be done by sheer human effort but by dependence on the grace and power he relied upon, which is equally available to every one of us.

Let's draw a comparison for a moment between Paul's type of Christianity and our own. Is this not humbling? As Christians we can too easily be lulled into thinking that our faith is there to construct comfort zones for us into which we can snuggle, protected from a dangerous world. Too often we simply want to be looked after and kept safe – in other words we want to be cosseted and pampered. This attitude is a far cry from that of the first Christians, for whom faith was bracing and life a challenge. Such an outlook requires a deep dependent trust and serious commitment, but let us not forget that, once we turn our lives over to Jesus, He supplies all we need. Keep in mind that Paul is not expecting us to match his gifts or achievements, but his passion for the one thing worth doing with our lives.

FURTHER STUDY

1 Cor. 4:16-17; 11:1; 2 Cor. 11:23-33

1. What was Paul's example?

2. Who was Paul himself imitating?

Wishing to emulate Paul, Oswald Chambers named his most successful book, *My Utmost for His Highest*. Raymond Edman said of Chambers that he was a man 'never content with low achievement ... always climbing the mountain peaks'. In the Alps there is a grave of a climber who died attempting to ascend one of the Alps' highest peaks. On the grave, after the climber's name, are these words: 'He died climbing.' May that be true also of us.

God, although I may not match Paul's gifts and achievements I can give myself as he did to the one thing that matters - the pursuit of Jesus and His love, making Him known among men and women. I do so now willingly. In Jesus' name. Amen.

Enemies of the cross

FOR READING & MEDITATION – PHILIPPIANS 3:18

'For, as I have often told you before and now say again even with tears, many live as enemies of the cross of Christ.' (v18)

Paul now turns the attention of the Philippians from himself and those like him who are passionately pursuing the things of God, to warn them about those who are on another path altogether. It's hard to know just who these people were whom Paul calls 'enemies of the cross'. That they are to be identified with the 'dogs' of verse 2 seems unlikely, but they were almost certainly other Christians of one sort or another! So why the dreadful description?

Perhaps these people, like some in Corinth, were engaging in overindulgences with food and shameful sexual conduct, falsely believing that such physical appetites could be indulged without damage to their spiritual life. Or perhaps they were simply opting for an easy-going version of the gospel rather than embracing the true gospel, which calls for long-haul discipleship marked by the cross in order to live life like Jesus. Neither the script of the story of Jesus' humble and self-giving servanthood nor that of Paul's renunciation of all things for Jesus' sake has any role for self-seeking stardom.

FURTHER STUDY

1 Cor. 11:17-22;
Jude 3-16

1. How were those in Corinth not on the right path?

2. What are the marks of enemies of the cross?

One thing is sure: it's extremely sobering to realise that anyone believing in Jesus Christ might be an enemy of the cross. Yet it seems there are such individuals among us. Those who emphasise triumphalism to the exclusion of suffering service, those who bypass the atonement and encourage attempts to reach heaven through self-effort, those who put happiness ahead of holiness, are 'enemies of the cross'. It would be good to pause and remind ourselves that any reduction of Jesus' gospel marks us as being not one of His friends but one of His enemies. A sobering thought indeed.

Help me, Lord, not to tamper with the truth. I tremble at the thought that I might become an enemy of the cross rather than a carrier of the cross. Let nothing ever bring me to that point. In Jesus' name I pray. Amen.

Dead ends

FOR READING & MEDITATION - PHILIPPIANS 3:19-20

'Their mind is on earthly things. But our citizenship is in heaven.'
(vv19-20)

Although Paul uses strong language when he talks of those who live as enemies of the cross, he weeps for them at the same time (v18). These are the only tears in the letter of joy, showing that Paul is torn apart by the thought of Christians living far below how God intended them to. Tragically turning all moral values and standards on their heads, they are indulging their physical appetites, idolising their bellies in the process! What they delight in is what Paul considers they should be ashamed of. Paul once more targets the mindset behind such behaviour. Their failure is that they set their minds 'on earthly things'. 'Earthly things' in this context are not the practical affairs of everyday life but things that characterise a worldly outlook that is in opposition to God.

In stark contrast to those whose horizon is limited by this world, Paul affirms that a true Christian's 'citizenship is in heaven'. James Moffatt's version reads: 'But we are a colony of heaven.' Though strictly not an accurate translation, this brilliantly catches the flavour of what Paul is saying and is an apt rendering because Philippi was a military colony of Rome. The Christians in Philippi knew they owed allegiance to a different Emperor and another kingdom.

Consider this question: Is my church, as far as I can make it, a colony of heaven? Is my home here in time, as far as I can make it, a settlement of eternity? Do Jesus' rules and customs prevail within its walls? Is service the motive, peace the atmosphere, joy the sunshine and love the energy? Remember, your residence may be in this world, but your real citizenship is in heaven!

FURTHER STUDY

Matt. 6:19-21;
Col. 3:1-3;
Heb. 11:8-16

1. What does it mean to be heavenly minded?

2. Contrast earthly and heavenly mindsets.

Father, thank You for reminding me of the fact that I am in this world but not of it. I belong to another King and another kingdom. Help me make my home a colony of heaven. In Jesus' name. Amen.

Because He lives

'And we eagerly await a Saviour from [heaven], the Lord Jesus Christ' (v20)

Paul now goes on to focus on the reasons why his, and our, focus is to be on heaven. This world has many imperfections and struggles that we constantly wrestle with, which is why we are longing for the return of the glorious Saviour Jesus who will one day take us to be with Him in heaven. Let's look at the first words from our two verses today: 'And we eagerly await a Saviour from [heaven], the Lord Jesus Christ.' The Caesars and other significant benefactors in the ancient world were in Paul's day appropriating the title 'saviour' for their own self-glory. But, as Christians, Paul reminds us that we are awaiting the return of the *true* Saviour, the only One who has broken the bonds of death.

FURTHER STUDY

1 Cor. 15:35-37;
Rom. 6:4-5;
8:11

1. What does our unity with Jesus mean for our future?

2. What does it mean for our present?

Take next the words 'who, by the power that enables him to bring everything under his control, will transform our lowly bodies so that they will be like his glorious body'. Just think of it: the body you now have, which is weak, prone to disease and perhaps at this moment wracked with pain or infirm through old age, is one day going to be changed into a body like Jesus Christ's body. And what kind of a body does Jesus have? Paul says a 'glorious' body. Because of Jesus' death and resurrection this is the sure and certain hope for all who die to themselves in Jesus.

Again, the match with Philippians 2:5-11 assures us that the Father's glory, which Jesus went through death to share, He will share with us, in turn, in resurrection. Our first creation body may be troubled by age and disease and give way to death, but our new creation body is guaranteed to be resplendent with glory – a body like Jesus' glorious body. Because He lives we shall live for ever. And how!

Lord Jesus, how I rejoice that Your endless life guarantees my endless life. One day I am going to be clothed with a body just like Your glorious body. Thank You dear Saviour. Amen.

Paul's crowning joy

'Therefore, my brothers, you whom I love and long for, my joy and crown, that is how you should stand firm in the Lord, dear friends!' (v1)

As Paul moves to his closing exhortations he expresses once more his deep affection for the Philippians. He addresses them very warmly as his loved and longed-for friends and family. 'My dear friends! I love you so much. I do want the very best for you' (*The Message*). Interestingly, there were various set patterns for letters in the ancient world, and Philippians has been identified by scholars as a classic letter of friendship. True friends and family, in the words of the writer Ben Witherington, 'love each other and look out for each other, including financially'. This is how it was between Paul and the Philippians. Furthermore, he calls them his 'joy and crown' – expressions that seem to look forward to the coming of Jesus. Paul, not wanting to have ministered in vain, hopes to meet Jesus with joy, pointing to the Philippians as the fruit of his labours. He hopes to 'wear' the Philippians like a victor's wreath, confident that they will be the reason he will not appear empty-handed before Jesus.

How remarkable that our lives are so bound up together as Christians. But reflect on the fact that it was for the joy set before Him of fulfilling the Father's will to save us that the Lord Jesus endured His shameful cross (see Heb. 12:2). It was with a view to being crowned with glory and honour as our truly human representative that Jesus tasted death for all of us. Remembering this will nerve us – as it nerved the Philippians – to 'stand firm in the Lord', knowing we are loved not just by His servants but by the Master Himself. And His love, unlike the best of human love, is a love that is guaranteed never to diminish, and never to change.

FURTHER STUDY

Matt. 5:43-48;
Luke 15:11-24;
Rom. 5:7-8

1. How did the father's love mirror God's love?

2. Contrast human love and God's love.

Lord Jesus Christ, You whose love never alters, help me to take comfort and confidence from this encouraging and reassuring revelation. Help me to rely on it even when I do not feel it. In Jesus' name. Amen.

Disagree well

FOR READING & MEDITATION – PHILIPPIANS 4:2-3

'I plead with Euodia and I plead with Syntyche to agree with each other in the Lord.' (v2)

When God raised Jesus to life, He put His stamp of approval on the mindset and lifestyle of Jesus, which had led Him not to look out for His own interests but to humble Himself and become obedient unto death for us. Paul vividly pictured this mindset in chapter 2, and commended it by his own testimony in chapter 3. It is this Christlike mindset that Paul now urges on two women in the church at Philippi who seemed unable to get along with each other.

From what we know of the social background, and from the fact that Paul mentions their names, we may conclude that they were two important women leaders in the church. Euodia and Syntyche had been Paul's co-workers along with Clement, and he encourages a particular colleague whom he trusted to bring about a reconciliation. So their disagreement is unlikely to have been a mere tiff but a serious dispute about how the gospel should be practised in Philippi. Perhaps one of them was opting for a safety-first policy by favouring returning to the social shelter of overt Judaism. Whatever the reason for their differences, Paul implores them to agree with each other in the Lord.

Notice that the apostle didn't ex-communicate or de-Christianise these women because they disagreed. He appealed to them both as being 'in the Lord' and said their names were in 'the book of life'. Being in the Lord does not always guarantee mental and emotional agreement. But when we embrace the mindset that is in Christ Jesus – the mindset Paul has said so much about in this epistle – then we can disagree without being disagreeable. If this speaks to you today bring it before the Father and ask for help.

FURTHER STUDY

Dan. 12:1;
Heb. 12:22-24;
Rev. 21:22-22:6

1. How does your name get into the book of life?

2. What will happen to those in the book?

Father, teach me when to stand straight and when to bend. And let me not be afraid to bend lest I be considered weak. The bending bamboo is stronger than the unbending pine. Teach me how to disagree without being disagreeable. Amen.

Rejoice *again*

FOR READING & MEDITATION – PHILIPPIANS 4:4

'Rejoice in the Lord always. I will say it again: Rejoice!' (v4)

Once again Paul encourages the Philippians to rejoice in the Lord, but this time he adds the word 'always'. In other words, rejoice in the bad times as well as the good times, the dark times as well as the bright times. The words 'rejoice' and 'joy' occur twelve times in this letter – a letter, we must not forget, that was written from prison. Dr E. Stanley Jones commented: 'Twelve lotus blossoms of joy come to the surface in this letter, rooted in the muck and mire of injustice. It is a joy "in spite of".'

The Christian faith is the most joyous faith in the world. It is not a Pollyanna type of religion that sees no evil; it sees the evil and recognises that God can turn evil into good. Buddhism looks at life and says: 'Life is suffering.' Christianity looks at life and says: 'Life is suffering – glory hallelujah!' Suffering can be transformed when God is invited into it. One preacher in an Easter Sunday sermon said: 'Many Christians have Easter on their calendar, but not in their character.' Those who have Easter in their character live out their lives knowing that Good Friday is not the last word – Easter is.

Have you noticed how psychologists are increasingly stressing the importance of joy? This is what one psychologist says: 'Nothing tones up the system as much as a constant flow of joy.' We might add: 'And nothing suppresses the system as much as a constant flow of sadness.' In Jesus life is joy. 'J-O-Y,' said a little girl in Sunday school, 'means "Jesus Over You".' Joy is more than a feeling, it is an attitude – an attitude characterised by the conviction that nothing can successfully work against us when we belong to Jesus.

FURTHER STUDY

Neh. 8:10;
Psa. 100:1-5;
Isa. 12:1-6

1. What is the root of joy?

2. What is the fruit of joy?

Jesus, You are joy, pure unalloyed joy – joy that bubbles up through every sorrow. I do not have to seek for joy when I have You. To have You is to have joy. My springs of joy are in You and never run dry. Amen.

Forbearance

FOR READING & MEDITATION - PHILIPPIANS 4:5
'Let your gentleness be evident to all.' (v5)

Paul wants the Philippians to be known for their 'gentleness'. It is not easy to translate this word accurately. Howard Marshall helpfully comments that 'The word suggests "magnanimity", the ability to remain reasonable and unperturbed when confronted by difficult people and to treat them calmly and fairly.'

Frank Thielman points to the use made of this word in the Jewish Book of Wisdom. Evil people who do not believe in the afterlife want to go out with a bang but meet opposition from a righteous man who disapproves of their irresponsible merriment. The evil people then decide to persecute the righteous man to find out how 'gentle' he is and to 'make trial of his for-bearance'. So, Thielman concludes, 'the term "gentleness" was often used of an attitude of kindness where the normal response was retaliation'.

FURTHER STUDY

Rom. 12:14-21;
Col. 3:12-14;
1 Pet. 2:18-23

1. Define and give examples of forbearance.

2. How can humans show Christlike forbearance?

The Anglican commentator Dr Handley Moule offers this as a translation: 'Let your yieldingness be known to all men.' Keeping in mind that Paul has just been talking about the problems that existed between Euodia and Syntyche, it is probable that this was the thought in the apostle's mind when he used the Greek word *epieikes*.

Be it magnanimity, forbearance, kindness or yieldingness, Jesus manifested each of these qualities in the highest degree as He refused to revile His detractors and persecutors (see 2 Cor. 10:1; I Pet. 2:23). What a wonderful change the gospel can bring about even in us to overcome any natural grumpiness. Whether tempted to lash out at those who are opposing us or to explode in exasperation with irritating people, the grace of God can and should produce in us Christlike reactions.

God, the more time I spend with Paul the more I come under the sway of his inspired words. You went into them and now You are speaking through them. Set me free to be what You want me to be and to live as You want me to live. Amen.

It's getting closer!

FOR READING & MEDITATION - PHILIPPIANS 4:5

'The Lord is near.' (v5)

How reassuring to be reminded that 'The Lord is near.' We can take this in two senses, as the Philippians no doubt would have done. On the one hand, 'The Lord is near' in that His second coming is looked for with eager expectation. Paul has constantly sought to lift the Philippians' eyes to the horizon so that they would live in the light of Jesus our Saviour's final arrival on the scene. He endeavoured to strengthen their morale with the conviction that the next important event to settle the course of human destiny would be the appearance of the Lord of history Himself. At the same time, 'to live is Christ' (1:21), and here and now we can know Jesus' presence with us. Maybe Paul deliberately lets the ambiguity stand. George B. Duncan, however, argues that the statement 'The Lord is near' relates very much to the difficulties between Euodia and Syntyche. Their estrangement, he suggests, would have been a topic of conversation. Paul, therefore, is saying: 'There is not only a problem in your church but there is a Presence – the *Lord* is near. Don't do anything to cause Him to withdraw.'

Whether or not Paul had in mind the words of the psalmist when he said, 'The Lord is near,' we cannot tell, but he certainly echoes words such as these: 'The LORD is near to all who call on him … in truth' (Psa. 145:18). Scriptures such as this would prompt the thought of prayer that Paul takes up in the very next breath.

Let us be glad that we can live confidently in the nearness of the Lord whether that is temporal or spatial. Either way, with the Philippians, we can rejoice, forbear and pray because the Lord we love is closer and nearer to us than we think.

FURTHER STUDY

Acts 17:24-28;
Heb. 10:19-22;
James 4:8

1. In what sense is the Lord always near to everyone?

2. How can we be nearer to Him?

Heavenly Father, help me to remember that I live every day in Your presence. The days come and go but there is never one when You are not with me. I am so grateful for this. Blessed be Your name for ever. Amen.

The sacrifice of praise

FOR READING & MEDITATION - PHILIPPIANS 4:6

'Do not be anxious about anything, but in everything, by prayer and petition, with thanksgiving, present your requests to God.' (v6)

To stop being anxious is easier said than done! Does Paul's command mean we are not to take forethought about anything? No, Jesus commended forethought (eg Luke 16:1–9). We gather all the information about an issue, pray over it and then make a decision in the light of God. Anxiety is the consequence of holding matters in our own hands and trying nervously to bring them together, depending only on our own resources. Forethought is good, anxiety is bad.

One doctor analysed his patients' anxieties in this way: 40 per cent were anxious over things that had simply never happened, 30 per cent were anxious about past events now totally outside their control, 12 per cent were unduly anxious about their health although their only illness, he said, was a diseased imagination. Ten per cent were concerned for their families although in most cases their qualms were groundless. Only in 8 per cent of the cases did the worries have a basis in conditions that could be treated.

FURTHER STUDY

Psa. 107:1-22;
1 Thess. 5:16-18

1. How are thanksgiving and petition linked in prayer?

2. What is God's will for us?

Paul's suggestion for anxiety is this: prayer *and* thanksgiving. The thanksgiving is the element that saves prayer from becoming *anxious* prayer. But how can we pray with thanksgiving when faced with situations that provoke anxiety such as serious financial difficulties or health problems? We can thank God because at the heart of even the most desolating trouble there is a mercy, since good can come out of it. In times of trouble, prayer *with* worship is not easy. The writer to the Hebrews refers to a 'sacrifice of praise' (Heb. 13:15) – praise that almost has blood upon it, believing in defiance of the God-denying look of things. The sacrifice of praise is indeed precious in God's sight.

Father, I have been focusing only on my troubles, forgetting that You will never desert me or forsake me. Help me to remember that – no matter what troubles me – and give thanks. I do so today. In Jesus' name. Amen.

FOR READING & MEDITATION - PHILIPPIANS 4:7

'And the peace of God, which transcends all understanding, will guard your hearts and your minds in Christ Jesus.' (v7)

Yesterday we considered the challenge of not being anxious about anything and how we can offer prayer with thanksgiving. C.H. Spurgeon once said: 'Some prayer lists are a recital of our unbelief. If we surround our needful burdens and petitions with as much thanksgiving as we can muster, then we will gain the courage to be quite specific with God about exactly what we want Him to do for us.' The result of prayer with thanksgiving, says Paul, is that we can experience supernatural peace – the peace and presence of God.

The Philippians lived under an all-embracing and repressive political regime – the Roman Empire. This prided itself on having subjugated the known world in order to bring to every nation the benefits of the *pax Romana*, the Roman peace. This Roman peace was maintained by garrisoning troops all around the empire to put down uprisings and to quell dissent. In the final analysis Rome kept its peace by the crosses it erected to execute those who disturbed that peace. Residents in the colony of heaven, however, are garrisoned in their hearts by heaven's peace. This heartfelt peace of God surpasses any merely natural way of understanding peace. The peace of God is an amazing confidence when everything else is falling apart; this is the peace of Galilee in a storm and Gethsemane in crisis. This peace, too, is established by the cross Rome erected on which Jesus died! Ray Anderson observes: 'Serenity is not being in control but being under control.'

FURTHER STUDY

Psa. 23:1-6;
John 14:27;
16:33;
Rom. 5:1-5

1. How can we experience God's peace?

2. Contrast the world's peace and Jesus' peace.

So today, whatever is disturbing you, pray with thanksgiving and experience the deep inner peace which the Holy Spirit imparts by whispering to your soul: 'I'm here in this with you.'

Father, how thankful I am that I have a heart that is guarded – guarded by peace. Because I have peace *with* You I am now able to experience the peace that flows *from* You. And this is a peace that never goes to pieces. I am so thankful.

A healthy mind

FOR READING & MEDITATION - PHILIPPIANS 4:8

'whatever is true, whatever is noble, whatever is right ... if anything is excellent or praiseworthy - think about such things.' (v8)

The list of virtues Paul gives in this verse could have been endorsed by many people in the ancient world. What this implies is put well by Frank Thielman: 'this list, with its admonition to look for the virtue in the wider world, reminds the Philippians that, although society sometimes seems hostile and evil, it is still part of God's world and contains much good that the believer can affirm.'

Understandably, this list has often been used by Christians on a moral crusade to clean up the media, stamp out pornography and so on. Such wrongs must, of course, be challenged, as a poisonous mental diet damages us both psychologically and spiritually. But this text should not be used only in a proscriptive, negative way. Looked at positively, it is a glorious invitation to explore every part of God's creation with childlike curiosity. Paul encourages us to let our imagination take wings and range over all the God-given landscape of loveliness and excellence. We should bear in mind that this verse follows on from his advice to stop being anxious. The more you focus on the common blessings of life, which are so commonly overlooked, the less anxiety will be able to take root in you.

FURTHER STUDY

Psa. 143:5;
Isa. 26:3-4;
Luke 12:22-31

1. Why are many people anxious?

2. What is the antidote?

So take time out, prayerfully and thankfully, to feel the fur of a cat, trace a shaft of sunlight, enjoy the smell of rain on mown grass, find the wisdom in an old woman's face, relish the magic of choral music, gaze with wonder at great paintings. You may discover that in a thousand ways in this fallen yet still beautiful world we can catch a glimpse of creation's glory and even now taste the goodness conceived in the holy, healthy mind of the Maker.

Once again, dear Lord, I must ask Your forgiveness for allowing my perspective to be jaundiced by the negatives so that I miss out on the positives. Help me every day to see the good in Your creation and to celebrate it. In Jesus' name. Amen.

NEXT ISSUE

The Presence of God

Do you feel God's presence every day, not just theoretically but in reality?

The Christian life is so much more than just following a set of rituals and traditions.

In this issue, Selwyn shares with us how we can practice knowing the presence of God and experience Him more powerfully in our everyday lives. Each day he unpacks how God not only wants us to know about Him but also to experience His presence and live the full life He designed us to have.

Every Day *with Jesus*

MAY/JUN 2016

The Presence of God

'You make known to me the path of life; you will fill me with joy in your presence, with eternal pleasures at your right hand.'
Psalm 16:11

Be revived and refreshed by God's Word   **CWR**

e Also available as eBook/ eSubscription

The God of peace

FOR READING & MEDITATION - PHILIPPIANS 4:9

'Whatever you have learned or received or heard from me,
or seen in me - put it into practice.' (v9)

Paul was apostle, spiritual father, friend and mentor to the Philippians. He wrote this letter straight from the heart. It was written out of love for them and to promote their spiritual progress. He has just urged them to fill their minds with good things; now he wants to remind them to *do*, as well as think, good things. *The Message* paraphrases this verse thus: 'Put into practice what you learned from me, what you heard and saw and realized.' It wasn't an academic, theological discussion; a cognitive treatise – it was a lifestyle achievable because they had seen it lived out by Paul.

FURTHER STUDY

Matt. 7:24-27;
John 13:17;
James 1:22-25;
1 John 2:3-6

1. Why is seeing and understanding the truth insufficient?

2. What is the result of obedience?

What the Philippians had learned from Paul was the full content of Christian instruction, the skills of how to walk and talk as disciples of Jesus. The great apostle was without doubt one of the greatest (if not *the* greatest) exhibitors of Christian belief and practice the world has ever seen. The Philippian converts had witnessed in Paul's way of life conduct that was perhaps as close to that of Jesus as it is possible to get. 'Men return again and again to the few who have mastered the spiritual secret, whose life has been hid with Christ in God.' So wrote Robert Murray McCheyne who, himself, well merits his place in that saintly category.

If the Philippians practise what they have heard preached by Paul and seen exemplified in him and in others then the God of peace, says the apostle, will be with them. And so it will be also with us. An old hymn puts it well:

When we walk with the Lord, in the light of His Word,
What a glory He sheds on our way!
While we do His good will, He abides with us still,
And with all who will trust and obey!

Gracious God, I know You will do Your part - help me to do mine. I don't just want to be just a hearer of Your Word, but a doer of it also. Take my obedience and work into it Your most excellent harmonies. In Jesus' name. Amen.

Ready for anything

FOR READING & MEDITATION – PHILIPPIANS 4:10-13

'I have learned the secret of being content in any and every situation'
(v12)

Paul's rejoicing here is different from his other 'rejoicings' in this epistle. The other rejoicings were general rejoicings over permanent relationships in the Lord. This one is over a specific thing – the Philippians' renewed concern for his welfare. 'Actually,' the apostle goes on to say, 'I don't need anything personally; by now I have learned to be content' (paraphrase).

Take first the words: 'I have learned the secret of being content.' This passage, said Dr E. Stanley Jones, 'gives an insight into the soul of the world's greatest Christian and an insight into the secret of his greatness. He had learned to take whatever came and make something out of it.' There are some who can stand plenty but not poverty, and there are some who can stand poverty but not plenty. Yes, that's true. Paul could take both poverty and plenty in his stride. Everything was grist to his mill. And the secret was this: 'I can do everything through him who gives me strength' (v13).

FURTHER STUDY

Prov. 15:16-17;
1 Tim. 6:3-19;
Heb. 13:5

1. What is the secret of contentment?

2. Why do some people experience many griefs?

Even as we enjoy the principle this contains, we must watch we do not take it out of context. This is probably one of the most abused texts in the Bible. Read in the light of the previous verses, 'all things' can refer only to things pertaining to Paul's apostolic ministry. In other words, empowered by Jesus, Paul has been able to cope with whatever life has thrown at him in the pursuance of his God-given commission. The 'everything' must not be interpreted as all the things we want to do but all the things God wants us to do. J.B. Phillips captures best Paul's thought in his translation: 'I am *ready for anything* through the strength of the one who lives within me.' That's joyous living.

Father, help me to go out into this day, and from now on, every day, whispering to myself: 'In the strength of the One who lives within me I am ready for anything.' Burn this truth deep within my heart I pray. In Jesus' name. Amen.

Giving and receiving

FOR READING & MEDITATION - PHILIPPIANS 4:14-17

'Not that I am looking for a gift, but I am looking for what may be credited to your account.' (v17)

Despite confidently assuring his friends that he is ready for anything through the strength of Jesus within him, Paul is concerned not to sound ungrateful for the gift the Philippians have sent him. 'I don't mean that your help didn't mean a lot to me – it did. It was a beautiful thing that you came alongside me in my troubles' (v14, *The Message*). Yet though he has learned the secret of contentment in any and every situation, Paul does not want to give the impression that he is a lone-ranger, a self-sufficient independent spirit who has no need of anyone else. That would be at odds with what he teaches elsewhere about the interdependence of Christians in the Body of Christ. So he recalls gratefully the earlier support the Philippians had given him when he left Macedonia. 'You were the only church,' he tells the Philippians, 'which shared with me in *giving and receiving.*'

FURTHER STUDY

Exod. 35:20-29;
36:1-7;
Acts 20:32-35

1. Why were the Israelites so generous?

2. Why is it better to give than to receive?

Here is the heart of Paul's joy in his fellowship with the Philippians. Generous giving and humble receiving oil the wheels of love in the Church, and flow over into praise to God. Paul is insistent that he neither needs (v11) nor seeks (v17) their support. He's not after their money. But he knows that such reciprocity builds up the Church in love and completes the joy of all.

The phrase 'credited to your account' is used not to suggest there was an investment value in what Paul received but that through their giving they received spiritual dividends. W.L. Rowlands, a great Welsh preacher, used to say: 'The best thing about giving is to be the one who gives.' There is more to giving than just the loosening of the purse strings; it produces also a loosening of the heart.

My Father and my God, help me understand even more clearly that the releasing of my financial resources to Your cause rebounds in the release of something deep within me and brings pleasure to Your heart. Amen.

'Hot money'

FOR READING & MEDITATION – PHILIPPIANS 4:18

'They are a fragrant offering, an acceptable sacrifice,
pleasing to God.' (v18)

'**M**oney,' it is said, 'is power.' That is a conclusion with which there can be no possible argument. But is it possible to hold money without being corrupted by the love of money? Yes, if we understand that we are stewards and not proprietors, and we regard our money as God's money. Also, that we understand what Jesus meant when He said: 'It is more blessed to give than to receive' (Acts 20:35).

Yesterday we saw how Paul encouraged the Philippians to believe that their material support for his own life was not, in itself, the point; it was, we might say, immaterial. What mattered was the fruit it bore in their lives as they gave and received. This was the interest on the gift that Paul sought. 'When we let go of money,' says Richard Foster, 'we are letting go of part of ourselves and part of our security. But this is precisely why it is important to do it ... It makes life with God an adventure in the world, and that is worth living for and giving for.'

FURTHER STUDY

1 Chron. 29:1-14;
Matt. 6:1-4

1. Contrast stewardship and ownership.

2. What causes God to accept or reject our gifts?

Paul goes on to say in this verse that the gifts they sent with Epaphroditus were 'a fragrant offering, an acceptable sacrifice, pleasing to God'. You are no doubt familiar with the term 'laundered money'. This is money fraudulently obtained. But fragrant money is that which no one has a tight fist around. In giving it with open hands and generous hearts, the Philippians show evidence of their fruitfulness in God's service. In receiving it with an open heart, Paul recognises their gift to him as one made to God – a sacrifice of praise. Such giving is a 'sweet-smelling aroma'. It smells good to God because it has been offered back to God on the sacrificial fire of the altar.

Once again, dear Father, I pray that You will prompt me to have an open heart and an open purse. May I see myself as a steward of Your resources and not the proprietor. Guide me in my giving and, above all, help me be generous. In Jesus' name. Amen.

The divine supply line

FOR READING & MEDITATION - PHILIPPIANS 4:19

'And my God will meet all your needs according to his glorious riches in Christ Jesus.' (v19)

Today we come to what is considered by many to be one of Paul's most powerful and inspired statements. The Bible commentator Gordon Fee describes this declaration as 'a master stroke'. It is one of the most oft-quoted texts of the New Testament. Eugene Peterson's paraphrase is a beautiful one: 'You can be sure that God will take care of everything you need, his generosity exceeding even yours in the glory that pours from Jesus.' Of course, the promise is not a blank cheque so that we might indulge our whims, but it is a cast-iron guarantee that God will meet all our legitimate needs. Our needs, remember, not our greeds. As soon as we were brought into the world our heavenly Father provided for our needs. Air to breathe? It was there for the taking. Milk? It was there in our mother's breast.

FURTHER STUDY

Luke 6:38;
2 Cor. 8:1-15;
9:1-15

1. How does God's supply line operate?

2. What does it depend upon?

Just as God has provided for our physical and emotional needs so He has provided for our spiritual needs, on a lavish scale: 'his glorious riches in Christ Jesus'. God is gloriously rich in resources and can be trusted to fund His work and take care of His people. 'When Paul says "riches in glory,"' said Alexander Maclaren, 'he puts them up high above our reach, but when he adds "in Christ Jesus," he brings them all down amongst us.'

Does this promise involve our financial circumstances too? Yes, if we understand the biblical principles of finance. Christian giving and receiving is part of the joyful supply chain that maintains God's investment in our world. No one is at a disadvantage by sacrificially supporting God's work. God is no one's debtor. He gives on a scale worthy of His wealth – 'the glorious riches in Christ Jesus'.

Father, I see this statement of Paul's is no casual comment. You inspired him to write it for it sums up Your divine intention - to supply all my needs. Help me not to misunderstand and make it mean 'greeds' rather than 'needs'. In Jesus' name. Amen.

Saints in Caesar's household

FOR READING & MEDITATION - PHILIPPIANS 4:20-22

'All the saints send you greetings, especially those who belong to Caesar's household.' (v22)

The thought of God's gloriously lavish giving moves Paul to a characteristic burst of praise: 'To our God and Father be glory for ever and ever. Amen.' It is as if Paul is punching the air – as winners do when they realise they have won. His final greetings flow from this exultant praise. Every saint in Philippi is to be personally greeted on behalf of Paul and those of his colleagues who are with him at the time of writing.

Intriguingly, Paul sends the greetings of 'saints … who belong to Caesar's household'. This phrase refers to members of what we would call the civil service or government administration – especially pertinent if the letter was written from Rome. Caesar's household was a place of intrigue, of lusts of the flesh and of lust for power. It was a veritable hive of ungodliness. Saintliness in the midst of that? Yes. The believers' bodies lived in Caesar's household but their spirits belonged to the household of faith. They absorbed Jesus' righteousness in the midst of unrighteousness.

Why does Paul particularly mention the saints in Caesar's household? Had they perhaps in their travels visited Philippi and become acquainted with the church there? Or perhaps, as Howard Marshall suggests, there was a 'Philippi prayer meeting' in Rome with a special burden to pray for the Philippian church. Whatever the reason, Paul's greetings give another glimpse of the extraordinary interconnectedness of all who love Jesus. A 'network of grace' is set up when Jesus changes our lives. If you are in a Caesar's household today then take heart. You can be sure God will touch someone's spirit to intercede for you.

FURTHER STUDY

2 Kings 5:1-19; Dan. 6:1-10

1. How would Naaman live in Aram but worship in Israel?

2. How did Daniel remain faithful in a hostile environment?

God, if I have to live in a little 'Caesar's household' where I am daily subjected to temptation, may I remember I belong to Your household. Help me live a heavenly life even when I am in a hostile environment. In Jesus' name. Amen.

Grace in the end

FOR READING & MEDITATION – PHILIPPIANS 4:23

'The grace of the Lord Jesus Christ be with your spirit. Amen.' (v23)

Paul's last message is one of grace. 'The grace of our Lord Jesus Christ be with your spirit.' Writing from prison we might have expected him to say: 'Grace be with me.' But no, it is 'Grace ... be with your spirit.' Such is the other-centredness of the great apostle that his thoughts constantly flow out to others. Paul needed grace in prison and the Philippians needed grace where they lived also.

Philippi was made a Roman colony by Octavian (Augustus) after a military victory in 42 BC. Now it was populated with freedmen and veterans from the Roman army. Nowhere outside Italy was there a city more thoroughly Roman. But, in the midst of Roman culture and imperialism, the Christians at Philippi were, as we saw earlier, living not just in a colony of Rome but also in a colony of heaven. Grace could not only turn a prison into a preaching centre (as it did for Paul) but it could turn Philippi into a settlement of eternity.

FURTHER STUDY

John 1:16-17;
Rom. 3:19-24;
Titus 3:3-7

1. Contrast the effects of law and grace.

2. What makes grace so amazing?

But let the last thought be of the amazing grace of our Lord Jesus who, as Paul told us earlier in the letter, did not exploit His advantages, but humbled Himself to become a servant and was obedient even unto death. It was that grace – grace flowing from Jesus – that turned a proud Pharisee into a Jesus-obsessed apostle. It is that grace, too, that makes us citizens of heaven's kingdom and raises our sights to a coming Saviour. What is more, it is by this transforming grace that He changes our death-ridden earthly bodies into radiant, resurrection bodies modelled on His. It's all grace isn't it? Grace upon grace. Can anything be more wonderful? Grace be also to you, dear reader, in Jesus' name.

Father, never let me forget that, like the apostle Paul, I am what I am by the grace of God. I have access to a reservoir that never runs dry. By grace I started my Christian life. Help me be ever open to it. In Jesus' name. Amen.